Compassionate Warrior Boot Camp for White Allies

By: David W. Campt PhD
@thedialogueguy
www.whiteallytoolkit.com

I AM Publications

Compassionate Warrior Boot Camp for White Allies
Copyright © 2018 by David W. Campt

All rights reserved. No part of this publication may be reproduced, distributed, or transmitted in any form or by any means, including photocopying, recording, or other electronic or mechanical methods, without the prior written permission of the publisher, except in the case of brief quotations embodied in critical articles and reviews and certain other noncommercial uses permitted by copyright law. For permission requests, please contact the publisher.

I AM Publications
(617) 564-1060
contact@iampubs.com
www.iampubs.com

Design & Layout By
Stephen Price
stephenprice-creative.com

Printed in the United States of America
First Edition, 2018
ISBN: 978-1-943382-04-0

Introduction

Introduction and Purpose

Congratulations for deciding to engage in the Ally Conversation Toolkit's Compassionate Warrior Boot Camp for White Allies. By engaging in the content of this journal, you are embarking on a journey that will likely positively impact your relationships over the course of your lifetime. What's more, your participation will enhance your ability to address one of the world's most pressing problems—racism. Kudos to you for your efforts to make the world a better place.

This journal will guide you to taking some important steps on your way to becoming a Compassionate Warrior for reducing racial hierarchies and divisions. The Ally Conversation Toolkit (ACT) uses the term Compassionate Warrior for a few reasons. First, the struggle against racism is a multi-front war, squaring off against the lower parts of human nature, against our societal conventions about how groups relate to each other, and against structures and systems that continue to reinforce the belief that some people are inherently more deserving than others because of the group they were born into. Many people who are on this journal have been committed to this process for years and know that this struggle has the complexity and breadth of a war.

But unlike many wars where the goal is to defeat "the enemy," the Compassionate Warrior takes the position that one way to engage in the war against racism is to focus on compassion for those who appear to be on the other side. From this perspective, the war is largely about freeing people from a blindness that is engulfing them, in other words, revealing the ways in which societal racism functions to blind a large number of people to its existence. How does this happen? People are persuaded that racial hierarchies in society and in their own heads are natural, or perhaps even what higher powers have ordained. If one has accepted this mindset, the people at the lower ends of the racial hierarchy become less deserving of compassion, respect, and even material resources.

Many anti-racism advocates find it hard to extend compassion to people who have racist views or who tend to deny racism's existence. It's a natural response to deny compassion to those who deny it to others. It turns out, though, that this response is not helpful. There is ample evidence from different fields of science that the best way to enhance the compassion of other people who lack it is to show compassion to those people.

So this initiative is for people who, in the war to dismantle racism, aspire to be both warriors for compassion and with compassion.

Premises of This Initiative

- Today, about 55% of white people believe that racism against whites is just as important of a societal problem as racism against people of color. The fact that so many whites hold this view is a problem that undermines America.

- Though they may be more difficult to execute, strategies for influencing people based on compassion and empathy are more likely to work better than those based on verbal combat, shaming, or other verbally aggressive methods.

- It is important for anti-racism allies to develop their own understanding of societal racism and awareness of how whiteness and other racial realities function. However, doing this internal work should NOT BE thought of as a necessary precursor to the work of effectively engaging others who don't think that racism against people of color is real and a problem worth addressing.

- Put directly: People who think racism is a problem should immediately start trying to influence others, even without additional reading, support groups, and training.

Compassionate Warrior Boot Camp

Premises and Cautions

There are several premises that this initiative is based on. Although you may not wholeheartedly agree with every one of them, having misgivings with some of them may inhibit you from benefiting from the processes suggested here.

Unless you believe the premises more than you question them, this process may lead to more frustration or confusion than clarity and useful guidance. If you are on board with the above, there are two additional points that are worth noting and remembering.

This Boot Camp only provides preliminary guidance. Just as in the military, a boot camp is merely an initial experience that prepares soldier for to begin learning the tasks that lie ahead of them. Learning to become effective at engaging people who are skeptical about racism is a life-long process; this is only the booster shot to that journey.

Moreover, the journey toward becoming a Compassionate Warrior against racism is one that has many dimensions. The focus of this journal is on one particular task—engaging people who question racism, something that is often neglected within the anti-racism discourse. **Please remember that engaging people who deny or minimize racism is not the only important task for anti-racism allies.** Others include: working on one's self-awareness, improving one's interactions with people of color, appropriately collaborating within liberation movements, building an interracial beloved community, among many others. So even if you dramatically improve your effectiveness, you should not declare yourself sufficiently woke and no longer in need of any additional self-improvement.

Some Additional Notes About Using The Compassionate Warrior Guide:

The purpose of this guide is to improve your ability to effectively and compassionately manage conversations with other people. In service of that, you will be guided to execute specific activities that involve interacting with others. If you have a socially isolated life circumstance (or a very introverted personality), you will face additional challenges in doing the exercises in the guide. These challenges will not be insurmountable; you will simply need to initiate short conversations with people in places like cafes and grocery stores. For the most part, you will be focused on developing your skills in asking questions and listening attentively. If you approach people pleasantly and signal that you only want a short conversation, the vast majority of people will talk to you.

The vast majority of the daily exercises are designed to take 20 minutes or less per day. One exception is Day 24, which will likely take about 45 minutes; it will also require you to engage a friend (a Boot Camp Buddy, which will be explained below) to help you.

There are many studies that suggest that if you practice a new behavior (including a new thought pattern) for 21 days in a row, you maximize your chances of making it a new habit. Thus, the best way to most effectively use this Boot Camp is to engage the material for 28 days in a row, as outlined. In the testing phase of the Boot Camp, a number of people who were enthusiastic about improving their allyship reported that the demands of life made it virtually impossible for them to actually devote 20 minutes a day to the activities. You might decide that you will more reliably complete the sequence by completing

Compassionate Warrior Boot Camp

Introduction | iii

the tasks every two days or at some other frequency. Whether your boot camp day is one calendar day, two calendar days, or some other duration, you will get the best results if you at least think about your allyship every day. In addition, please do the tasks of boot camp days in order; they have been sequenced as a progressive behavioral curriculum.

For a few of the exercises, it will be helpful to work with a friend who supports you putting energy into improving your allyship. Early in the process, you will be asked to identify one or two who might serve as your Boot Camp Buddy. It is best if this person is also engaged in this process too, but at a minimum, they need to not oppose this process as an aspect of your personal growth. You should consider keeping them appraised of your ongoing progress on or just after your weekly reflection and synthesis day, so they feel connected to and invested in your development.

The exercises are all aimed at increasing your ability to engage both people you know and people you don't know in conversations about race/racism. We recognize that engaging people whose racial views you don't know will feel like a stretch for some people, especially those who lean toward introversion. If you have to push past a disinclination to engage strangers, remember that the core task you are doing is extending compassion, and thus increasing the amount of compassion in the world.

This Compassionate Warrior Boot Camp is formatted to allow for you to take notes on your experience every day. Doing so will significantly aid your progress. But if the time demands of your life make the journaling expectation feel burdensome, it is more important to do the exercises. The weekly journal entries can partially make up the gap in reflection if you can't make some reflection notes every day.

Boot Camp Key Facts

- In the testing phase of these exercises 70 percent of the people spent completed the tasks in less than 25 minutes per day, and 55 percent in less than 20 minutes per day.

- For most days, the bulk of your time will be spent on doing the exercise, not on reading. There are a few exceptions. Day 1 introduces you to the sensibilities and approach of the initiative, and has the most reading of any day. Days 4, 7, 13, and 28 have less reading than Day 1, but more than most days. For the most part, the reading level is very light.

- Once every seven or eight days, the daily task will focus on not talking to people, but rather will focus on your making mental and written reflections of your recent progress.

- Some of the activities are not explicitly directed to issues related to race, but will help you get ready to have encounters that are race related.

- Each day includes "Expected" activities that should take no more than 20 minutes. On a few days, there are "Bonus" activities that might take up to an additional 20 minutes.

- Increasing your ability to act from a place of empathy and compassion on racial issues is highly likely to help your interactions with people that concern other topics.

Compassionate Warrior Boot Camp

"If you want others to be happy, practice compassion. If you want to be happy, practice compassion."
—*Dalai Lama*

Date   /   /

Day 1
Understanding The ACT Compassionate Warrior Approach

"Racism springs from the lie that certain human beings are less than fully human. It's self-centered falsehood that corrupts our minds into believing we are right to treat others as we would not want to be treated." —Alveda King

Today will be the only day in the boot camp that will be primarily focused on reading.

> ### Today's Objectives
> - Read this overview about the core approach of this initiative.
> - Make a list of racially problematic statements you've heard.
> - Make a list of people you know with problematic views

Background: The Compassionate Warrior Approach

The Compassionate Warrior Boot Camp is based on the finding that conversational approaches using respectful dialogue, empathy, and story telling are more effective in influencing people compared with conversational styles that emphasize factual information, debate, combat, and shaming people.

A critical task for influencing people is to remain calm and centered, and not emotionally activated when disagreement on the issues occurs. It is valuable to have pre-rehearsed strategies that you can use to calm yourself if necessary. It is also helpful to have self-management strategies that you can invoke during the conversation to help you regain a centered and calm place if you begin to stray.

One primary reason that factual information does not work well when trying to persuade people around deeply held beliefs is due to something called the Backfire Effect. This psychological dynamic works as follows: When people are confronted with facts that contradict deeply held beliefs, the tendency for the vast majority of people (from all ideological perspectives) is simply to discard the facts as "fake news" and recommit themselves to their beliefs. When people feel that someone is challenging deeply held beliefs, the part of the brain that is activated is the same part that is engaged when people perceive physical threats.

A key strategy in getting people to re-visit their points of view is to first establish a sense of rapport with them and get them to see you as someone who is like them, not someone in an opposing group.

Compassionate Warrior Boot Camp

Day 1

One way of building rapport—even if someone has just made a statement you find problematic—is to ask them to say more about their point of view, even if it's something as simple as saying, "Tell me more about that." Ideally, you want them do more than restate their belief; you want them to reveal underlying factors, such as their deeper values or experiences. Focusing on values is usually better than talking about beliefs. The best strategy is to focus the conversation on the personal experiences that have been notable in shaping or reinforcing their beliefs.

Having them talk about their experiences helps activate a part of the brain called mirror neurons, which puts us in other people's shoes and often mimics the feelings that we think the other person had during the experience they are recounting. This approach helps build rapport.

Once you have demonstrated your interest in their experiences, you are in a position to leverage another common psychological dynamic. Because of something that many mammals have called the Reciprocity Principal, if you listen to someone's anecdote, most people will feel obliged to listen to an anecdote from you. Then, when you tell a personal anecdote, you have a chance to fire up the other person's mirror neurons, further enhancing rapport.

To solidify rapport, the first story you should tell should be one that they naturally empathize with. Your goal is to get them nodding along with your story and identifying with the idea that you and they have similarities.

After you establish a sense of rapport, you are in a much better position to try to influence them. Once they trust you and do not see you as the enemy, it is best to relate an experience that has influenced the way you see the issue at hand (in this case race/racism).

> The sequence above can be summarized as the RACE method of managing a conversation. RACE stands for
> **R:** Reflect—get ready for the conversation
> **A:** Ask about their experiences
> **C:** Connect—relate a personal story they will find partially affirming of their viewpoint
> **E:** Expand—relate a personal story that invites them to a new understanding of the issue

Some Additional Points About the RACE Method:

People do not like the feeling that you are running a program on them. Your goal is to become facile enough with the process so that it feels natural and not stilted.

Often, people will respond with queries about why they believe what they believe with "facts" they have heard from the media. Sometimes, you will have to give them extra encouragement to get them to focus the conversation on their actual lived experiences. This might look like: "I bet those facts wouldn't ring true if you did not have an experience that confirmed them. That is what I really want to hear about. " Or, "I trust people's experiences much better than media reports, since there is so much bad media out there. I want to know what you have personally seen about this."

There are people whose views about race are so entrenched or their conversational style is so toxic that it does not make sense to engage them. As Dr. Eddie Moore of the White Privilege Conference says, "There are some pancakes that cannot be flipped." While Compassionate Warriors are bold and open to difficult tasks, they also recognize that it is important to not waste energy on people who are beyond reach.

People who think that racism against people of color is a problem worthy of specifically addressing are called "anti-racism allies," or merely "allies." Clearly, there is a broad spectrum of intensity, focus, and commitment among allies. Some allies devote their entire lives to promoting racial equity, whereas some are just barely on the good side of the 45%/55% split. Many projects and writers focused on inclusion emphasize these distinctions, such as distinguishing between allies, advocates, accomplices, and activists. In some contexts, these differences are important. Since this boot camp focuses on empowering and equipping anyone on the ally side of the divide to more effectively engage racism skeptics, this document will only spend minimal time on categorizing distinctions between different levels of allyship.

> ### Terminology
> The ACT initiative uses the term "racism skeptic" to refer to the 55% of white Americans who don't believe that racism against people of color is a problem worthy of addressing. Although this initiative does believe that these people are denying something for which there is overwhelming evidence, the initiative does not refer to them as "deniers," since they would very likely find this term disrespectful, and disrespecting people is at odds with showing them compassion.

ACT's Take on the Foundational Issues

With its multiple offerings, the Ally Conversation Toolkit initiative is designed to help white allies have better conversations with racism skeptics in a wide variety of circumstances. For example, if you read the full 298 pages of the White Ally Toolkit Workbook, you will have reviewed specific material relevant to conversations about race and police, the belief that people of color are lazy, the idea that racial oppression was too long ago to talk about, and a host of other topics.

This boot camp is less comprehensive on the number of specific racially problematic statements it prepares you to address. Our goal here is to introduce the basic sensibility and methods of the initiative as well as to give you some usable tools to navigate the most foundational topics in the disconnection between allies and skeptics. This foundational disagreement, from the perspective of this initiative, is the persistence of systemic unconscious bias and the notable racial progress that has been made in recent decades.

About a third of the way through this experience, you will begin to focus on delivering your personal stories that will equip you to implement the Connect and Expand phases of the RACE method. Before then, you will be working on vital skills – relaxing, asking questions, and listening - that you will need in order to deploy these stories effectively. Still, it is useful to make you aware of the topics of those stories, so that your unconscious and semi-conscious mind can begin probing your memory for experiences that will become the basis of the personal anecdotes in your toolkit.

This initiative takes the position that of all the many dimensions of the disconnections between white people who see racism differently, there are two deficits among allies that are most important in blocking effective communication.

1)   Allies are not skilled and comfortable in relating stories that might identify areas where the ally himself or herself is still sometimes subject to having their thoughts and/or actions affected by unconscious racial biases.

Compassionate Warrior Boot Camp

4 | Day 1

2) Allies are not skilled in telling stories that support that idea that significant racial progress that has been made over the past several decades. This skill has not been developed largely because anti-racism allies fear making concessions about racial progress will support racism skeptics' denial and minimization of on-going racism.

Because these issues are foundational to the disconnect between allies and skeptics, this boot camp will give you encouragement to develop your own personal stories about unconscious bias and about racial progress. The hope is that by the time the boot camp is over, you will have in your toolkit at least two pithy and compelling stories about the way that even you sometimes have racially biased thoughts. In addition, the aspiration is that by the end of the boot camp, you will have two pithy and compelling stories that explain why you believe that there has been some notable racial progress over recent decades. When interacting with racism skeptics, your racial progress and unconscious bias stories will serve as Connect and Expand stories, respectively.

> The exercises in the boot camp will not focus on these stories until Day 7. But for those who want to get started early, feel free to let your mind start percolating on these questions:
> - What is a moment you had that demonstrates that you still are subject to thinking thoughts that reflect an unconscious racial prejudice/bias, even if only briefly?
> - What is a moment when you observed something that demonstrates to you that there has been notable racial progress in the past few decades?
>
> If you find yourself resisting these ideas, don't worry. We will return to these ideas later. Still, to maximize your experience, we suggest that you assume the questions are based on something that is true, even if part of you wants to raise objections.

Day 1 Tasks

Part 1: Racially Problematic Statements You Sometimes Hear

What are four statements that you've heard from other white people that you think are racist or racially problematic? Don't describe the statements; write them as you've heard them. Put them in quotation marks.

1.

2.

3.

4.

Compassionate Warrior Boot Camp

Day 1 | 5

Part 2: Racism Skeptics in Your Circle of Influence

Think about people in your extended circle of contacts who are likely be racism skeptics. That is, they would likely be among the 55 percent of white people who would say on an anonymous survey that they think that racism against whites is just as important of a social problem as racism against whites. Also, try to remember something they said that makes you think they are a skeptic.

Name of Racism Skeptic	One statement they made that reflects that they are a skeptic
1.	
2.	
3.	
4.	
5.	
6.	

Part 3: Potential Boot Camp Buddies

Think about two people who can be your Boot Camp Buddy. This is someone who may not be doing the boot camp, but who would be supportive of your working on your compassionate communication skills in service of dismantling racism. A few times during the boot camp, you will want to borrow a little bit of their time to run stories by them and get feedback. On Boot Camp Day 24, you may ask them to do a role play exercise. It is best if both of you are in the same room, but the most important thing is that you have a good relationship that is supportive of your efforts to grow in your allyship.

Potential Buddy #1

Potential Buddy #2

Before too long, you may want to talk to your buddies and tell them about your need of their support in the next 29 days. Once they say they are willing to support you in this way, checking in with them now and then will likely increase their investment in your progress.

Compassionate Warrior Boot Camp

Day 2
Learning Quick Relaxation Methods And Listening Tips

Date / /

"A mind at peace, a mind centered and not focused on harming others, is stronger than any physical force in the universe." —Wayne Dyer

To make good choices in conversations with skeptics, it is useful to enhance your ability to relax just before or during a tense interaction. In addition, it is useful for everyone to discover techniques that will help them become a better listener.

Today's Objectives
- To choose and begin experimenting with a fast-acting relaxation method.
- To choose and begin experimenting with a behavior that enhances your ability to listen.

Background

Even if you already have your own rapid relaxation practice, you are encouraged to try some of the ones presented below. The big picture message is this: One factor that will affect your capacity to execute Compassionate Warrior methods is your level of centeredness and relaxation in the face of racially problematic situations. Thus, part of the goal of the boot camp is to encourage you to mentally and emotionally link empathetic listening methods with the relaxation methods.

Below are short descriptions of four different relaxation methods that have been promoted as capable of providing benefits after three minutes of engagement. After reading them over, notice which ones you are drawn to. You should first do the one that stands out the most, but we suggest that after a couple of days, you try some of the other ones. Sometimes people find that a method they did not think would be helpful turns out to be so.

Part 1: Choose a Relaxation Method, Try It, and Notice How Well It Works.

For all of these exercises, it may be valuable to set a timer for three minutes.

1. Deep Breathing and Noticing Thoughts

Get in a relaxed sitting position in the quietest place that is convenient to access. Try to focus on your breathing. When you inhale, think "I am"; when you exhale, think "at peace." As extraneous thoughts come in—and they almost certainly will—notice them, gently push them aside, and return attention to your breathing.

2. Imagine a Relaxing Spot and Go There

Pick a setting that you find relaxing—whether it is someplace you have already been or someplace that you can imagine. Spend the first 15 seconds establishing a pattern of relaxed breathing, then close your eyes and shift your attention from your breathing your preferred location. Imagine as many details as about it as possible, but don't pressure yourself to create the clearest mental picture. Focus on the things about the setting that relax you, whether it's the sights, sounds, smells, sensation of the air, or something else. Imagine that you are there, and try to live in the relaxation that this place fosters within you.

3. Progressive Body Relaxation

During this exercise, you will slide your attention all over your body. At each major body part, take note of how tense or relaxed the part is and briefly try to relax it. Notice how it feels, then move on to the next. Start with your toes and feet, then move up to your ankle, calf, going ever higher and making sure your focus on both sides of your body.

4. Self Massage

(This is from Giovanni Zanoni, Massage Therapist at on-demand massage service, ZenNow.)

Close your eyes. Using your index and middle fingers, make small circles on each temple. Let your fingers walk up your hairline, making small circles along the way, until they reach the middle of your forehead. Then have them travel down until you reach your eyebrow line and make the same circles outward as you head back to your temples. Since hands can carry a lot of tension (especially for heavy keyboarders), do the following: use the thumb and forefinger to massage the soft area between the thumb and index finger. Do one hand with the other and then switch.

Your task for today is to choose one of these methods and use it over the next four days, starting today. Today and at least for the next 10 days, whenever you do one of these relaxation methods, make a note (mental, written, or on a device) about how well the method worked.

Part 2: Review a List of Listening Tips, Then Choose Two to Practice Today.

Below is a list of Listening Tips that anti-racism allies have said can be helpful when trying to be an empathic listener. Today's list focuses on the mind-body connection. (This is not the last list of tips you will see during the Boot Camp.) Make a note of the two that you think might work best for you.

1. **Biting one's lip**
2. **Touching your tongue to the roof of your mouth**
3. **Shifting your position to one that is more relaxed**
4. **Taking deeper breaths**
5. **Keeping your eyes focused on the speaker's eyes**
6. **Imagining there is glue on your lips, preventing you from talking**
7. **Keeping your eyes focused on the speaker's mouth**

If you have a Listening Tip not on this list, be sure to add it. On today's worksheet, there is a table that can house your reflection notes about how well the listening tips worked in conversations.

Compassionate Warrior Boot Camp

8 | Day 2

Day 2 Tasks

Part 1:

Choose one of the following three-minute relaxation methods.
1. Deep breathing and noticing thoughts
2. Imagine a relaxing spot and go there
3. Progressive body relaxation
4. Self-massage

At some point during the day, execute the method, and make a mental note of the answers to these questions.

1. What is your level of relaxation/tension at the start of the exercise?
2. How much did the exercise help you move toward greater relaxation?
3. Note any other observations about the experience of using the method you chose.

Part 2:

1. Choose two of the following Listening Tips to use today.
1. Biting your lip.
2. Touching your tongue to the roof of your mouth
3. Shifting your position to one that is more relaxed
4. Taking deeper breaths
5. Keeping your eyes focused on the speaker's eyes
6. Envisioning there is glue on your lips, preventing you from talking
7. Keeping your eyes focused on the speaker's mouth8. (Your own tip)

2. Try one tip at two different points today.

3. Assessment

Compassionate Warrior Boot Camp

Day 2

	Topic & Person	My listening performance from 1 to 10 with "10" as the highest
Which Listening Tip _____		
Which Listening Tip _____		

Which of these best describes the impact of the Listening Tip on your performance as a listener?

	Listening Tip 1 _____	Listening Tip 2 _____
Very helpful		
Somewhat helpful		
Not helpful/Not distracting		
Somewhat distracting		
Very distracting		

Reflections:

How well did the relaxation methods work? What are you key takeaways from your experience with them?

How did the listening tips work? Key takeaways from your experience of them?

Compassionate Warrior Boot Camp

Date / /

Day 3
Asking Questions That Focus On Experiences Beneath Beliefs

"If you do not know how to ask the right question, you discover nothing." —W. Edwards Deming

A core task within the RACE method is asking people questions to get them talking about their experiences. By the end of the boot camp, this should be easy. We will start today with beliefs that are NOT ones you disagree with.

> **Today's Objective**
> Ask two people to relate experiences they've had that affect their beliefs.

Background

Your goal today is to ask at least two people about an experience that might lie beneath a belief they have.

If in your typical day, you have encounters that could accommodate people sharing a brief anecdote with you, then just look for those opportunities.

If in your typical day, you do not have encounters with people that could accommodate brief storytelling, you may need to go out of your way to create such an encounter. Before you ask people for an experience that lies beneath their belief, you may need to remind them of a previous conversation when they revealed this belief to you.

Please note: The exercise is still valuable if the belief you ask about is not about race. In fact, you may want to purposely ask about a belief that is about something very benign and **not likely** to get their or your emotions going. The point of today is NOT to get into an exchange about race relations; it is to give you practice in directing someone's attention in a conversation from their belief to an experience that is related to that belief. (This is also an opportunity to practice one or more Listening Tips and take note of their impact on you.)

Two Common Ways of Asking Experience Questions Are:

1) Asking about a Recent Experience that validates their belief: "I find that viewpoint interesting. Can you tell me about a recent experience you had that confirmed for you this way of seeing things?"

2) Asking about a Past and Formative experience that helped form their belief: "I was thinking about that conversation we had last week. Remember when you told me that you think *(blank)*. Can you tell me when you first started thinking that way and what you experienced that caused you to realized that? I would love to hear about that."

Compassionate Warrior Boot Camp

Day 3 | 11

Day 3 Tasks

Part 1: Planning

- Say each of the question types out loud twice in the mirror to find a way of phrasing them that feels natural.
- Decide whether you might need to make a specific effort to contact people or if your day will likely provide opportunities to ask about experiences.
- If necessary, mentally clarify whom you might specially contact and think about how and when you might do that. Think about the topic you want to ask them about.
- Think about which Listening Tip you will use when it's time to listen to the answer to your question.

Part 2: Execution

- If possible, ask someone for an experience twice during the day. If you can, use both the recent and formative experience ways of asking strategies.
- When the moment arrives, use one of the listening tips presented yesterday.
- Notice how comfortably you can pose each of the question types.
- When the moment is over, make a mental (or written note) about your experience.

Reflections

How did the two experiences compare, regarding:

- Asking the question
- Invoking the Listening Tip
- Actually listening to the person

Your Assessment (on a Scale of 1-10) About How Well You:

	Recent experience question	Formative experience question
Asked the question		
Used the Listening Tip		
Made the person feel heard		

Additional Reflections

Any additional takeaways? Also, for practice, try to ask someone for a story every day.

Compassionate Warrior Boot Camp

Day 4
The Apologetic Non-Apology

"It is wrong and immoral to seek to escape the consequences of one's acts." —Mahatma Gandhi

Discomfort in talking about race has harmed many relationships between anti-racism allies and racism skeptics. There are people who don't go to family gatherings to avoid repeating a past contentious conversation about race! It is time to heal such breaches.

One key task of Compassionate Warriors is learning and mastering skills for being an active agent of healing where there has been tension or a disruption in the past. When these disruptions happen, there is usually one person who is more at fault, and everybody plays a role. It is particularly important that we are able to hold ourselves accountable for things that we ourselves have done to harm relationships – even if an objective analysis would assess our behavior is the smaller portion of the blame for the disconnect. The good news is that we can often initiate a healing process simply by owning up to our piece of the problem, regardless of what the other person does.

Today's Objective
- To learn about a conflict resolution tool called the Apologetic Non-Apology (ANA)
- To make some initial planning steps in anticipation of doing an ANA

Background

Today is the first of several sessions during the boot camp that you will make progress on something called the Apologetic Non-Apology (ANA). This is a method for having an encounter where you name and take responsibility for your own behaviors or thoughts that have been harmful to relationships.

(Like all of the methods in the boot camp, we will not jump into the deep end of the pool right away. We will start slowly and make incremental progress).

The ANA represents a statement where the speaker 1) conveys misgivings about their role in a previous encounter, and 2) conveys whatever vulnerability they feel in the moment as they have the conversation, and 3) expresses a commitment to try to avoid repeating this behavior.

When doing an ANA, a Compassionate Warrior (or anybody) holds themselves accountable for the behavior in the past that was not helpful to connectedness to the other person. But the person doing the ANA does not issue an apology, nor try to extract an apology from the other person. Apologies are important in healing relationships. However, managing an apology transaction has complications; such interactions can go off the rails and wind up re-injuring relationships. An ANA involves one person simply holding themselves accountable for their misdeeds, without the expectation that the other person will admit anything. Thus, this process has much less risk of causing unintended negative outcomes.

The Ana Has Three Elements:

1) **Past/Accountability:** Recall the topic of the previous conversation and name the behavior (potentially including your thoughts they don't know about) that was not helpful to building a connection with the person. This may be as subtle as mentally labeling someone's point of view "silly" during the conversation.

Examples of ways to describe your unhelpful behavior:

- **Superior** •**Dismissive** •**Accusatory** •**Rude** •**Not Listening**
- **Withdrawn** •**Petulant** •**Talked Over You** •**Acted Like A Know It All**

2) **Present/Vulnerability:** Name an emotion based in vulnerability that you are feeling in the moment as you refer to this prior incident

Examples:

- **Embarrassed** •**Nervous** •**Anxious** •**Ashamed**

3) **Future/Commitment to Improvement:** State your commitment to not repeating the problematic behavior. As a optional additional step, you can get the other person's buy-in by asking if it is okay if you ask them about their experience if the topic comes up again.

Note: you are highly unlikely to get a "no'" answer to this question.

Two Examples of What an Apologetic Non-Apology Might Sound Like Are Below:

ANA Example #1

Remember two weeks ago at the barbecue when we talked about the NFL players? I was thinking about it and I realized that I was **dismissive** of your perspective. I actually feel **a little embarrassed** now when I think about this. Our relationship does not need that, so **if we talk about the NFL players protest again, I am not going to act in this way**. Also, is it okay if I ask you about your personal experiences that are related to your viewpoint?

ANA Example #2

A few months back we were talking about poverty, and I was recalling that conversation recently. I realized that during that conversation **I talked over you a lot**. I have to admit that I am **somewhat nervous** just bringing this up now. I want to say that **I don't plan to do that in the future**, and I want to say that if we ever talk about that topic again, I will try to ask you about what you have seen that makes you see the situation like you do. Is that all right?

(Bold indicates the key elements of the ANA).

Note that the ANA does not have to be about race/racism. The conversation that your ANA revisits can be about any topic where you took actions or had thoughts that were unhelpful to your connectedness to someone.

Compassionate Warrior Boot Camp

14 | Day 4

Day 4 Tasks

Step 1: Preparation

The first step in delivering an Apologetic Non-Apology (ANA) is to prepare for it in advance. It is useful to be as clear as possible about the topic you were discussing, what you did that tended to harm connectedness, and how you think you will feel about it when you bring the prior moment up to the person you were talking to.

By the end of the boot camp, you will be encouraged to do an ANA with someone with whom you have had a difficult conversation about race. That is the end of our on-ramp; today is just the beginning.

For today, the task is to think about someone with whom you have done or thought something unhelpful to connectedness in a non-racial conversation. You will also answer the following questions and then practice saying the ANA in the mirror.

Question 1: What was the conversation about?

Question 2: How would you characterize the behavior, thoughts, or action that you engaged in? How did they affect the connectedness the two of you share?

Question 3: How do you imagine you will feel when you actually do the ANA with the person?

You can complete the ANA by simply declaring your commitment to not doing the unhelpful behavior again. The next question is for situations where you want to go further with getting your conversation partner's buy-in by asking them if it is okay to handle a future conversation differently.

Question 4: How would you form a question that lets them know that in the future, you would like to ask them about their experiences related to the topic?

Compassionate Warrior Boot Camp

Step 2: Execution

After jotting down answers to these questions, practice the ANA in the mirror.

	Incident 1/Person 1	Incident 2/Person 2
Topic		
What do you think you did that undermined connection?		
How you think you will feel when talking about it?		
How you would describe what you don't want to do again?		
How would you phrase the questions getting permission to ask about their experience if the topic comes up again?		

After you fill out the table, practice ANA in the mirror for each skeptic.

Reflections

What was your emotional reaction as you answered the preparation question?

How did it feel to practice the ANA in the mirror?

How easy or difficult is it to imagine actually doing the ANA with the person?

Bonus Activity:

There is an Apologetic Non Apology explanation and example on the ACT website.

Compassionate Warrior Boot Camp

Day 5
Focus On Your Connection With Skeptics In Your Circle

"Every problem emerges from the false belief we are separate from one another, and every answer emerges from the realization we are not."
—Marianne Williamson

As we work toward engaging people with problematic racial views, it is important to work on compassion for those whose views we abhor.

Today's Objective
Spend time thinking about your sense of connectedness with people you know who are racism skeptics. (If you don't know any full-blown skeptics, you can focus on people who whose views on race trouble you.)

Background:

As discussed on Day 1, the RACE method is based on influencing people by building rapport with them, then inviting them to revisit some of their racial views. To do that, it will be important to get past the natural inclination of many allies to focus exclusively on the ways they feel disconnected from racism skeptics. A step in this direction is to simultaneously hold in your mind their problematic beliefs along with things about them that might enable you to make a connection. That is today's assignment.

Day 5 Task

Review your list from Day 1 of the racism skeptics in your circle. (Some previous boot camp participants have said they do not have any skeptics in their circle. If this applies to you, for today and until the end of the boot camp, let the term "racism skeptic" stand for allies whose views on race don't quite agree with yours.)

From your list, choose the two skeptics whose views bother you the most. It is important to choose two people for the exercise.

Day 5 | 17

Do Your Best to Answer These Questions for Each Person.
Do One Person at a Time.

1. Identify the groups your skeptic seems to have the most prejudice against. (If the person is not a skeptic, write down the two specific racial issues in which their views are most problematic to you.)

2. What is an example of something they said that really bothered you?

3. What are 1, 2, or 3 other issues on which their views bother you? (Remember, this is not something you just disagree with.)

4. Think of the moment when you felt close to them.

5. Think of three things that you would say are admirable about them.

6. Think of three things that you have in common with them.

Bonus:

7. Can you think of something that you did during a race/racism conversation with this person where you did or thought things that were unhelpful to establishing connectedness? Jot a few notes down about this moment. (We will come back to this before the end of the boot camp.)

Compassionate Warrior Boot Camp

18 | Day 5

Day 5 Task Worksheet

Name of Skeptic:	Name of Skeptic:
Groups they seem to have the most prejudice against.	Groups they seem to have the most prejudice against.
Example of something they said that bothered you.	Example of something they said that bothered you.
If they exist, what are other issues in which their views bother you? Also note if you don't know if they have any other views that trouble you.	If they exist, what are other issues in which their views bother you? Also note if you don't know if they have any other views that trouble you.
Briefly write a phrase or sentence that referred to the time you felt closest to them?	Briefly write a phrase or sentence that referred to the time you felt closest to them?
What are three things that are admirable about this person?	What are three things that are admirable about this person?

If you can't think of actual racism skeptics, focus on people whose views on race bother you, even though they might be allies.

Compassionate Warrior Boot Camp

Reflections

How easy or difficult was it to fill out the worksheets? Were some parts of it more difficult to complete than others?

What thoughts or emotions came up for you as you completed the questions?

Did answering the questions change your perspective about having a conversation with the skeptics?

Compassionate Warrior Boot Camp

Date / /

Day 6
Finding Ideas You Like Embedded Within Perspectives You Don't Like

"He who cannot put his thoughts on ice should not enter into the heat of dispute." —Friedrich Nietzsche

A key skill for Compassionate Warriors is training the mind to find at least one idea within someone's perspective that you can agree with and use to build rapport. This is the first of a few days during the boot camp for practicing this skill.

> ### Today's Objective
> Watch a news channel with a perspective you disagree with for at least 10 minutes. Write down a point of agreement you have that is embedded within a perspective that is expressed on the news channel.

Background

The RACE method is the core of the Compassionate Warrior approach. This method of managing a conversation is based on the strategy of emphasizing at least one point of connection/agreement with a racism skeptic before trying to invite them to a new way of thinking. Because you have a sense of the kind of statements you hear most frequently or that bother you the most, you can prepare in advance for these encounters. A useful task is to review specific racially problematic statements and clarify ideas within them that you can align with.

Even if you do this, racially problematic statements will come up that you don't expect, so it is important to be able to respond in the moment. Today's exercise attempts to begin training your brain to look for some idea embedded in a perspective you disagree with and find something you can agree with.

One participant has described this process as "Looking for the chocolate in the trail mix."

When engaging someone who has said something that you find problematic, finding that chocolate in the trail mix means finding one statement that might allow you to say: "I may not agree with (problematic idea), but I do share your belief that (embedded point of agreement).

Here are a few examples from the White Ally Toolkit and from Fall 2018 headlines:

"I may not agree that very few people are racist any more, but I do share your belief that a lot fewer people are explicitly bigoted than a few decades ago."

Compassionate Warrior Boot Camp

Day 6 | 21

"I may not agree that police always treat people fairly, but I do share your belief that there are many good police officers out there. "

"I may not agree that Brett Kavanaugh is a suitable for the Supreme Court, but I share your belief every allegation against a nominee for an important position must not be automatically believed as true without investigation."

"I may not agree that separating families at the border is a good idea, but I share your belief that it would be unwise to have a policy of completely open borders."

Note: These examples are not meant to imply that you need to agree with these specific embedded points.

Day 6 Tasks

1. Spend 10 to 15 minutes taking in a national news roundup on a network that you tend to disagree with. If you are a progressive, Fox News Channel will likely serve the purpose. If you a centrist or conservative, MSNBC or a show like Democracy Now will work well.

2. As you listen, try to distill an important belief that is behind a story. THE IDEA DOES NOT HAVE TO BE RACE RELATED. This should be a perspective that you think most fans of the show would unabashedly agree with.

3. Try to find an idea that is embedded within this perspective that you can agree with. Write down the idea in the previously mentioned format: "I may not agree with XXXX, but I share your belief in YYYYY."

Pay attention to whether any emotions come up for you as you do this exercise. If they do, make a note of them. Remember, this does not have to be a racial issue for you to get value from exercising your brain in this way.

Compassionate Warrior Boot Camp

22 | Day 6

Day 6 Worksheet

- Take in information from a news roundup that is from a source that you usually disagree with.
- Listen carefully for 10 to 15 minutes. Jot down editorial perspectives within the stories that you tend to disagree with.
- Try to find at least one idea embedded within the perspective that you find agreement with.

Perspective you disagree with #1 I do not agree on that:	Embedded idea you agree with But I do share the belief that:
Perspective you disagree with #2 I do not agree on that:	Embedded idea you agree with But I do share the belief that:

Reflections

Did you have any reaction to doing this exercise that is worth noting?

Are there racially problematic statement issues that you hear that you cannot imagine finding some embedded idea you can align with?

Compassionate Warrior Boot Camp

Day 7
Your Experience Of Unconscious Bias

Date   /   /

"Fortunately for serious minds, a bias recognized is a bias sterilized."
—Benjamin Haydon

A key part of your arsenal as an anti-racism ally is being able to tell a compelling anecdote in which you witnessed a moment when a white person was operating on an unconscious bias. It is best—although not absolutely necessary—if that person were you. Today's task is to start developing this key tool in your arsenal. To help you get you started on developing your tool, today's assignment contains a greater amount of reading than is usually the case.

Today's Objective
Read some background information about unconscious bias, and then begin preparing a story about your being a witness to unconscious bias.

Background

ACT has engaged more than 2,000 people in workshops since spring 2017. During that process, we've found that most white allies have witnessed unconscious bias. They are uncomfortable talking about it, but an important step to unlocking your memories is changing from thinking that having a bias is a moral crime to accepting it as an inevitable part of modern life. The consensus among researchers who study unconscious bias is that the most important step in getting past bias is to admit that you have it to yourself.

Fortunately, there has been an explosion of written and on-line resources about this issue in the past few years. For those who need a primer on this topic, one contribution by the ACT team is Overcoming Bias, by Tiffany Jana and Matthew Freeman (Both Tiffany and Matthew have collaborated with ACT).

Most anti-racism allies are reasonably familiar with some basic facts about unconscious bias, the most important of which is that unconscious bias based on group membership is such a widespread phenomenon that it might be thought of as universal.

A core challenge when discussing bias with skeptics comes from the way that "racism" and "prejudice" are thought about—which is that they only reflect conscious and intentional bigotry. Since relatively few people harbor such feelings, many people proclaim themselves bias free because they do not understand that bias can be unconscious and nevertheless affect their thoughts and behavior.

Compassionate Warrior Boot Camp

24 | Day 7

Making matters worse, since they don't see any conscious bigotry in their own hearts and minds and that of the people they know, many people extrapolate that society is now essentially free of prejudice and racism. Thus, they process claims about racism as so much whining and excuse making, or even as cynical attempts to extract concessions and resources made by people who don't want to work hard.

One re-frame of discussions about bias that is often productive is to make the case that people often have unconscious bias against their own group. This re-frame makes bias not a function of group animus, but rather an insidious societal force that affects everyone.

Here are some brief pieces of data that illustrate the fact that unconscious bias can push people to have negative views of others in their own group.

- In one study, approximately 1,200 university professors (800 males, 400 female) who ran science labs were sent a resume of a hypothetical applicant for an entry-level lab assistant position. They were asked to rate the competence level of the applicant on a scale from 1 to 5 and to list the appropriate starting salary. All of the scientists were sent the exact same resume, except that half of the applicants were named Jennifer Smith and half named John Smith. Overall, John's projected salary was 15% higher than Jennifer's, and his competence assessment was 20% higher than Jennifer's. Significantly, there was no appreciable difference between the ratings by the female and male professors on the level of anti-female bias.

- In an analysis of the Implicit Association Test—an on-line test of unconscious association—about 30% of African Americans demonstrated an easier ability to associate white faces with positive attributes than black faces.

- In a 2010 study of 133 children that was sponsored by CNN, children ages 4 to 5 and 9 to 10 were shown images of white-skinned and brown-skinned dolls and were asked to associate them with positive and negative words. (This was a reprise of a famous 1947 doll study by Dr. Kenneth Clark.) Both white and black children showed a significant preference for white dolls.

- The following is a quotation from Jesse Jackson from the mid-1980s where he reflects on the way that he is subject to having an anti-black bias. "There is nothing more painful to me at this stage in my life than to walk down the street and hear footsteps... then turn around and see somebody white and feel relieved."

At some point, it may be useful to cite such facts in your attempt to influence a racism skeptic to believe that unconscious bias is a real factor. However, do not make the mistake of making facts into your core persuasive strategy. What is more effective is your own personal testimony about your witnessing a situation in which you saw unconscious bias at work. Most effective will be a story where the person having this bias is you.

Today's task is to take some notes about a few incidents when you observed that unconscious bias might have at work. In several days, you will turn one of these incidents into an anecdote that you will polish, practice, and at come point convey to others.

Day 7 Worksheet

Take some notes in response to these questions. It is not necessary to develop a full anecdote; for the moment, it is fine to write now, simply write enough to remind yourself of each incident. Later in the boot camp, you will review this list and choose one or more of these incidents to develop a full anecdote.

Question 1: Can you think of an experience where an unconscious or semi-conscious negative racial bias affected your own thoughts or actions—even if only very briefly—in a way that was out of alignment with your values?

Incident #1 when you think a negative racial bias was affecting your thoughts/actions?	Incident #2 when you think a negative racial bias was affecting your thoughts/action?

(If you have notes on two incidents, you can stop here, though we recommend you finish the form if you have enough time. If you don't have two incidents, continue completing the rest of the form.)

Question 2: Can you think of an experience when someone behaved toward you in a way you did not like and that you think was affected by an unconscious racial bias?

Incident #1 where you were the target of unconscious racial bias.	Incident #2 where you were the target of unconscious racial bias.

Question 3: Describe one or two incidents when someone behaved toward you in a way that you did not like and that you think reflected an unconscious bias that was not based on race—perhaps gender, age, location, accent, nationality, or something else.

Incident #1 when you were the target of unconscious non-racial bias.	Incident #2 when you were the target of unconscious non-racial bias.

Question 4: Have you ever you observed an interaction between two or more people where you think that unconscious bias (racial or not) was affecting the interaction?

Incident #1 when you observed bias operating between others.	Incident #2 when you observed bias operating between others.

Reflections

Did you have any emotions of note while reviewing your experience and looking for bias?

What are you other observations or lessons from participating in this exercise?

Compassionate Warrior Boot Camp

Day 8
Reflection And Synthesis

It's on the strength of observation and reflection that one finds a way. So we must dig and delve unceasingly." —Claude Monet

About once per week, you will be encouraged to use your 20-minute Compassionate Warrior time to reflect on your journey over recent days.

Today's Objective
Create written answers to the following questions.

What were the top takeaways that you have from the past seven days of boot camp activities?

Reflections

If you had to present it in a nutshell, what would you say you have learned about:

Your relaxation practices?

Your listening inclinations and skills?

Your relationships with racism skeptics?

Your ability/willingness to search for agreement with those whose views you disagree with?

Your perspective on unconscious bias?

Are there notable insights that you want to keep in mind as you progress to week #2?

Date / /

Day 9
Experimenting With New Listening Tips

"There are people who, instead of listening to what is being said to them, are already listening to what they are going to say themselves."
—Albert Guinon

Becoming a better listener is a core part of increasing your influence on people. Today's focus is on experimenting with different approaches to improving your listening practice.

Today's Objective
- Identify and practice two Listening Tips that you will experiment with over the next week.
- Engage a person who likely agrees with you and practice attentive listening
- Make note of how the listening tips affected you

Background

In previous boot camp activities, you were encouraged to use Listening Tips that focused on the mind-body connection. For the next several boot camp days, you are encouraged to practice Listening Tips that focus on managing your own thoughts.

Many people have found these strategies helpful in boosting their own compassion when talking to people they disagree with about controversial topics. The good news is that these methods are compassion boosters in any situation. Thus, you can try them out over the next several boot camp days, even if you don't have conversations with strong disagreement about race/racism.

Here are some methods that initiative participants have said can be useful at the beginning of or during a tough conversation about an issue where there is disagreement. Clearly, these methods can also be used when the conversation is not contentious.

1. Mentally picture the person as the vulnerable child they once were.
2. Remind yourself that the listening process you are doing is part of a long-term change process.
3. Remind yourself of qualities you like about the person you are talking to.
4. Think back to a time when you wanted to be listened to.
5. Think about things you have in common with them.
6. Think about helpful values you hold, such as empathy, curiosity, and/or patience.

Compassionate Warrior Boot Camp

28 | Day 9

Day 9 Tasks

1. Choose which of the methods for relaxing, asking questions, and maintaining your listening that you will use today.

2. Sketch out a plan for when you will use that particular method.

3. Execute your plan

4. Make a mental note of how well the tip worked immediately, and make some more detailed written notes later.

> Note: It is best if you use today as an opportunity to not just listen attentively, but to practice the skill of taking in someone's point of view and not offering yours in response. To maximize your chance of doing that, the suggestion is that you NOT focus on a topic that is highly controversial. After the person finishes explaining their experience, you can thank them, and say you want to think about what they have said. If the person appears to feel uncomfortable, offer your perspective, including an experience related to it.

Day 9 Worksheet

Planning

- Which relaxation method do you plan to use before you approach them?

- Which listening tip are you going to do?

- If you have an idea about whom you plan to engage today, note who they are below.

- Whom do you plan to engage?

- As you try to shift them from belief to experience, do you plan to ask them about a recent experience or a formative experience?

Execution

1. Find two opportunities to engage your Listening Tip.

2. Pay attention to what you are hearing AND the effects of your Listening Tip on you.

Reflections

Encounter #1

Who and what was the person and the belief that you inquired about?

Person

Belief you asked about

How would you describe how you asked them about their experience?

Compassionate Warrior Boot Camp

How smooth was your attempt transition them from belief to related experience?

☐ Very Smooth | ☐ Smooth | ☐ Kinda Smooth/Kinda Clunky | ☐ Clunky | ☐ Very Clunky

Listening Tip (check one)

Before the encounter: ☐ Did it | ☐ Kinda did it | ☐ Didn't do it

During the encounter: ☐ Did it | ☐ Kinda did it | ☐ Didn't do it

How much did the listening tip help you?

☐ A lot | ☐ A good amount | ☐ Some | ☐ A little | ☐ None/it distracted me

How much do you think they felt really heard? They:

☐ Felt very heard | ☐ Felt heard | ☐ Felt kinda heard | ☐ Did not feel heard

Encounter #2

Describe the person and the belief that you inquired about.

Person

Belief you asked about

How would you describe how you asked them about their experience?

How smooth was your attempt transition them from belief to related experience?

☐ Very Smooth | ☐ Smooth | ☐ Kinda Smooth/Kinda Clunky | ☐ Clunky | ☐ Very Clunky

Listening Tip (check one)

Before the encounter: ☐ Did it | ☐ Kinda did it | ☐ Didn't do it

During the encounter: ☐ Did it | ☐ Kinda did it | ☐ Didn't do it

How much did the listening tip help you?

☐ A lot | ☐ A good amount | ☐ Some | ☐ A little | ☐ None/it distracted me

How much do you think they felt really heard? They:

☐ Felt very heard | ☐ Felt heard | ☐ Felt kinda heard | ☐ Did not feel heard

Compassionate Warrior Boot Camp

30 | Day 9

Reflections

How did it feel to approach a conversation(s) with a focus on listening?

How did the experience of engaging people in this way compared to what you expected?

Any other lessons or takeaways from doing the exercise?

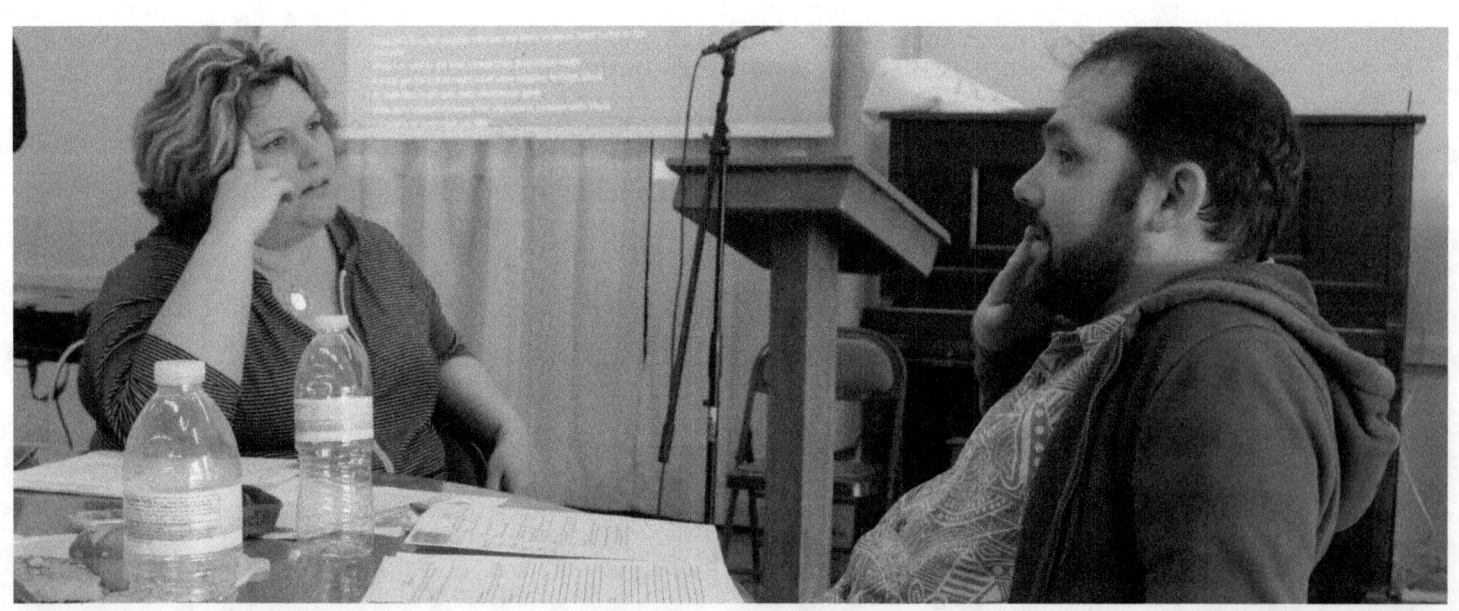

Compassionate Warrior Boot Camp

Day 10
Listening To Someone You Disagree With

"There is a difference between listening and waiting for your turn to speak." —Simon Sinek

Today is the first day where you are going to purposefully engage some with whom you disagree. Your engagement will simply be asking them an experience question about some belief they have, and listening to them without arguing, and exiting the conversation.

Today's Objective
- To practice using a relaxation method before a conversation you know may test you.
- To practice asking about the experiences of a person with whom you disagree.
- To practice a Listening Tip and assess its affect on your ability to listen and make someone feel heard.

Background

The task today is to purposely have a conversation with someone who has a belief you disagree with, and to practice asking them for an experience that animates their belief. Of course, you will also practice listening to their experience with the intention of making them feel heard.

It will be important to resist the temptation to have an argument with them about the belief. In fact, they might want to draw you into such an argument.

To increase the chances of you resisting the temptation to argue with them, it is probably best if the topic that you focus on is NOT something that triggers you. It is best to choose a topic with which you hold mildly differing thoughts. This way, you can test how well the relaxation methods and Listening Tips are helping you.

It might be best if the topic is a public issue that you have only moderate concern about. You may also choose an issue you have strong feelings about but is not as weighty; for instance, maybe you know they like a restaurant that you find terrible. The most important thing today is to engage the exercise and not avoid doing so because you can't find the perfect issue.

Again, choose a topic and a person that your ability will simply listen and not argue will be tested, but such that doing so will not make you feel like doing a disservice to yourself or a cause you care about.

Compassionate Warrior Boot Camp

Day 10

Here is a broad outline of how this conversation might go:

You: *(calmly, since you just did one of your relaxation methods)*: Remember when we had a conversation about *(the topic)*.

Them: Yes

You: It came to my mind the other day. I realized that I wanted to ask you more about your experience related to *(the topic)*. I hope that is okay.
Here is my question: *(Here you choose an experience question style [recent or formative]. Use your empathetic inquiry tone of voice, ask a question about a recent or formative experience related to their beliefs about the topic. Then listen with the intention of making them feel heard.)*

Them: *(they tell an experience related to the topic)*

You: I think I get it. Let me feed it back to you. One time, you *(summarize their experience.)* And that experience is related to why you think *(summarize their belief.)* OK, I think I see where you are coming from now. Thanks a lot for that. It really helps me to hear people's experience so that I better understand their perspective on things. Thanks again.

Note: If they push you to try to tell you what they believe or the experiences behind it, you may need to say something like this:

You: Thanks for asking about my point of view. I would be happy at another point to talk about my perspective on this issue, including my experiences that led me to see it how I do. But right now, what I really want to do is to focus on your experience, let that wash over me, and not fill my head with my own perspective. Can I get back to you on that at a different time?

Remember: There is a good chance that during or after they tell you their experience, they will make a link to their belief that you will find irrational or otherwise spurious. If this happens, IT IS IMPORTANT TO RESIST THE TEMPTATION TO ARGUE. Prepare in advance for this possibility. Have a plan for the Listening Tip that you will use to stay focused on your goal, which was to practice asking an experience question, practice a Listening Tip, and make them feel heard.

As soon as you can after the encounter, answer the questions on the worksheet.

Compassionate Warrior Boot Camp

Day 10 Worksheet for Reflections

- Did you try a relaxation method before the encounter? If so, how much do you think it helped you?

- Which Listening Tip(s) did you try, and when did you do them?

- Which style of asking questions did you implement? How would you rate the smoothness of your inquiry?

- How well did you listen? What lessons do you walk away with about how to improve your own listening practice?

- Were you able to resist the inclination to argue? If not, what might you do in the future to resist that temptation? If you did not argue, did you take any measures to help you resist the temptation?

- Did you get any value from actually listening to them, outside from strengthening your listening muscle?

- Any other important takeaways from this experience?

Compassionate Warrior Boot Camp

Date / /

Day 11
Planning An Apologetic Non-Apology

"A meaningful apology is one that communicates three Rs: regret, responsibility, and remedy." —Beverly Engel

Today's Objective
Become more comfortable with the Apology Non-Apology (ANA) method

Background

The goal today is to go a bit further than last week with the Apologetic Non-Apology.

The task is to use the ANA method with someone with whom you have had a disagreement that is not about race.

On Day 4, you filled out the ANA for someone with whom you had a disagreement that wasn't necessarily about race. Today's task is to do the same thing, but to choose someone who it would not be very difficult to have an encounter with in the course of a typical day.

It is possible that the person you used for your ANA last week is someone you will see in the natural course of the day. If this is true, choose a different person for today's exercise.

Your goal is NOT to try to create an encounter that has the significance of a deep and weighty apology, but rather is a semi-weighty acknowledgment of an error you committed. The goal is to do a slight reset of your communication pattern, not to perform a big *mea culpa*.

Think about someone whom you are likely to run across today and with whom you have had a conversation in the past year where you did or thought something that was unhelpful to connectedness. When you are clear about your person, use the Worksheet to prepare the ANA and to later capture your assessment of how the experience went.

Day 11 Worksheet

To prepare the ANA, answer these questions.

- What was the topic and setting of the conversation where you thought or did something that was detrimental to connectedness?

- What did you think or do that was unhelpful to connectedness?

- How do you imagine feeling as you bring this up?

- What is an honest statement you can make about not doing this again?

- What is an experience question that feels reasonably natural that you might articulate if you wanted to open the topic again?

As you think about this, think about how to execute this task. These questions might be helpful to think through.

- Will it be helpful to you to consciously relax yourself first? What method will you use?

- Will you need to pull the person aside, or will that add more drama to the encounter than is helpful?

- If they decide to tell their experience of the moment instead of just hearing from you, which Listening Tip will you use so that you make them feel heard?

Now that you have prepared for this encounter, practice the ANA in the mirror.

Do the ANA sometime today.

Compassionate Warrior Boot Camp

Day 11

Below are some evaluation questions for use after you have done the ANA.

How did the experience feel? Did you do the ANA?

What is your assessment of how the other person felt during and after the encounter?

Is there anything that you might have done differently?

What are the overall lessons from this experience that you want to remember as you think about using this technique in the future?

Day 12
Reflecting On Racial Progress

"The only thing more irritating that white people who say that everything has changed, is black people who say nothing has changed."
—John Lewis

As noted on Day 1, this Boot Camp will focus on the topics that are the most fundamental to disconnects between allies and skeptics. These topics are unconscious bias and racial progress. You have already begun preparing a story about unconscious bias. Today, your attention will turn to the issue of how to talk about racial progress over recent decades.

> **Today's Objective**
> To begin developing your story about racial progress, which will be a connect story for racism skeptics.

Background

If you are at all steeped in progressive racial discourse, you are likely to have been exposed to the idea that the level of racism today has not actually lessened in the past 50 or 60 years. Rather, this discourse sometimes asserts, racism has not declined—it has merely evolved and shape-shifted.

Since this point of view is rather common in progressive circles, you as an ally may be reluctant to talk about improvements in racism for fear that you will be harshly criticized for not being "woke" enough to see the reality of how racism is.

This initiative takes a different view about how America's ongoing racial predicament should be discussed. ACT takes the position that while racism remains a horrible problem that undermines the United States in innumerable ways, there is ample objective and anecdotal data that indicates racism has substantially declined in the past five to six decades, and even in the past two to three decades. Moreover, this initiative takes the position that admitting this progress to racism skeptics who deny the persistence of racism actually **strengthens** your ability to get them to concede that racial problems remain.

Specifically, there is significant value in your agreeing with a racism skeptic that America's racial situation has improved, and connecting with the skeptic using a personal anecdote that illuminates why you think this is true. After you do that, you will be much more convincing when you tell an additional anecdote that substantiates your belief that the nation still has racial problems.

If there is a part of you that wants to resist this approach, the suggestion is that you trust the curriculum, stay with the boot camp process. At that point, having developed and tested your Connect and Expand stories, you can test whether the above analysis is actually true.

Compassionate Warrior Boot Camp

Day 12 Worksheet

Your task today is to begin developing a story about racial progress that you will at some point use to connect with a racism skeptic. Your goal is to develop an anecdote that reinforces the point that there has been notable progress in recent decades, perhaps even within your lifetime. Look over the following questions and pay attention to which questions resonate with you.

1. If you ever did, when did you first notice that you were receiving messages that encouraged you to see some people of color as "other"? (These messages may have come from family, friends, the media, or other sources). What were some of these messages?

2. What have you experienced that lets you know that there is less bigotry now than there was just after the civil rights movement, or between now and when you are a child? What changes have you seen in your lifetime?

3. If possible, recall a story about witnessing explicit racism that you think would be much less likely to happen today because of different social norms.

4. During your childhood, were you exposed to an adult who tried to teach you to be racist in a way that would not likely happen today? If so, jot some notes about your memories about this.

5. If you have a second hand or observational story from at least 20 years ago from a person of color who experienced explicit racism in a way that you imagine would be much less likely to happen today, write down the key elements of that story.

If any of the above prompt questions resonates with you, jot some notes about experiences related to any of the questions that have at least some resonance.

After you have reviewed all of your notes, begin thinking about which incident(s) might be suitable as the centerpiece(s) of a short anecdote.

Reflections

Did you have any notable reactions – positive or negative – to the assertion that there has been racial progress in recent decades that is notable?

What was your reaction to the idea that allies are often not comfortable talking about racial progress and that talking about this issue is a potentially skill for allies?

Are there any other notable takeaways from the experience of reviewing your memory for experiences that suggest racial progress?

Compassionate Warrior Boot Camp

Day 13
Turning Notes Into Usable Anecdotes

Date / /

"Tell me the facts and I'll learn. Tell me the truth and I'll believe. But tell me a story and it will live in heart forever." – Ancient Proverb

Today, you will turn notes you have taken on unconscious bias and racial progress into bite-size anecdotes that you begin practicing.

Today's Objective

Using your notes from Day 7, create an anecdote about unconscious bias.

Using you notes from Day 12, create an anecdote about racial progress.

Background

On Days 7 and 12, you took some notes on personal incidents related to unconscious bias and racial progress, respectively. If your thinking about these issues has evolved since those days, you should add your reflections below. What directly follows is an brief overview of the structure of an anecdote and two illustrations.

Creating an Anecdote

A simple way of thinking about an anecdote is that it has three elements:

Setup: Context setting, with enough description of the physical, emotional, or social environment so that the listener can identity with you. If it is suitable, construct the setup so that it is not obvious what the key takeaway will be.

Key moment: This is the heart of the story from an observation/experience perspective. It could be something that the central figure in the anecdote thought, something they observed, some action they took, or something that happened to them. Usually, the key moment is not the exact same thing as the takeaway (below), but they are closely related.

Takeaway: Not unlike the moral to children's story, this is the overarching lesson, learning, or conclusion from the experience. Ideally, this is at least somewhat different from the key moment, but the lesson and the key moment should be constructed so that many if not most reasonable people would leave the experience with the same takeaway.

Compassionate Warrior Boot Camp

Here are two brief examples of anecdotes that allies have conveyed to ACT:

Set UP: I had heard about a food place that served chicken gizzards on the other side of town. I love gizzards, so I went to it. The place was in a mini-mart attached to a gas station on the black side of town. When I pulled up and parked, I noticed these two middle-aged guys drinking 40 once beers out of bags sitting near the door. They acknowledged me as I left my car and started to approach the door.

Key Moment: As this happened, my mind flashed on the idea that I needed to lock my doors, despite the fact that I could see the cook and the counter through the window, and would never be out of sight of my car. The cook was happy and surprised to see a white person coming for her food and we had a great conversation about the joy of gizzards. She named me "Gizzard Girl" that day and still calls me that when I come back.

Takeaway: The gap between the basic politeness of the guys with the beer and the niceness of the cook and my own completely unjustified fears of theft were very striking, and even embarrassing to me though no one but me knew what I thought. I guess certain prejudices are just deeply ingrained. And I have spent a lot of my career working in black communities!

Set up: I grew up in Northwest Indiana. I remember going to elementary school with a black boy named Kelsey (this was early 1980s). He was the only non-white student at my school, and his family was the only non-white family in the area. To me, he was like any other kid on the block, only with darker skin.

Key moment: I later learned that he was harassed at school, his family's house and cars were vandalized, and a group from a nearby Baptist church burned a cross on their front lawn. They were forced to move out of the area due to threats of violence.

Takeaway: I do not think this would happen in that area today. If it did, it would be a big social media story. So I guess this shows some progress.

To construct your anecdote on unconscious bias, you should refer to your notes from Day 7. If you have any additional reflections on your experiences with bias since you took those notes, write them below.

Note: The most convincing anecdote will be one where you noticed yourself having a bias towards another person. If you don't have one of those, but have one or more bias stories in the other categories (you being a victim of bias or you witnessing bias operating between tow other people) think through which of these would likely be most credible to a person who tends to believe unconscious bias does not exist.

Additional notes on your experience of racial bias:

In addition, if your thoughts about racial progress have evolved from Day 12, make some notes about this also so that your anecdote about racial progress can be as strong as possible.

Preparing Your Anecdote on Unconscious Bias

Set up: What are the key broad elements and specific details that help bring the listener to the situation?

Key moment: What is the moment when the bias became clear to you and would have to most people in the same situation?

Takeaway: What is the central idea about bias that stays with you from the experience?

Preparing Your Anecdotes About Racial Progress

Set up: What are the key broad elements and specific details that help bring the listener to the situation?

Key moment: What is the moment when notable racial progress became clear to you and would have to most people in the same situation?

Takeaway: What is the central idea about racial progress that stays with you from the experience?

Compassionate Warrior Boot Camp

Day 13

Execution

- After you take some initial notes and refine them, practice your stories in the mirror.
- Do each of them at least twice, at different lengths.
    - One version should be less than one minute.
    - One version should take up 2-2.5 minutes without boring the listener.

Reflections

What was your level of comfort telling your anecdotes?

Was your comfort level the same for each topic?

Did the duration you were focusing on affect your comfort level in telling your stories?

Are there any adjustments that you want to keep in mind as you think about telling these anecdotes in the wild?

Today is a day when you can do some extra skill building work.

Bonus Assignments:

During the course of the next 24 hours, tell someone – preferably someone who IS NOT a skeptic – your unconscious bias story.

Tell someone your story about racial progress.

After relating your stories, ask them if they have any experiences that tend to affirm or dis-confirm your takeaway from the story you told.

Compassionate Warrior Boot Camp

Date / /

Day 14
Relaxing And Telling Your Stories

"We so complex, we're mysteries to ourselves; we're difficult to each other. And then storytelling reminds us we're all the same." —Brad Pitt

The primary goal today is to begin experimenting with one-minute relaxation methods. A new one is being introduced to you. Now, you have five different methods to choose from from through the course of the week. The suggestion is that you do the one-minute exercise once in the morning, as well as just before the conversations that you will initiate.

Today's Objective
1. To experiment with a new relaxation method.
2. To rehearse you Connect and Expand stories.

Background

To boost your growth in the toolkit methods, the next several days of the Boot Camp will emphasize the way in which you interact with other people where disagreement will likely arise. In such cases, it is important to further refine your ability to get centered and stay centered. Here is where practicing one-minute relaxation methods, which are short of enough that you could conceivably excuse yourself and engage the method in a bathroom or private area just before the interaction you are preparing for.

In addition, you will continue ramping up toward using your racial progress and unconscious bias stories in the wild. Today you will practice telling them both in the mirror.

Compassionate Warrior Boot Camp

Part 1: Try a New Relaxation Method

Through the course of the week, keep experimenting with the quick relaxation methods from last week, except now do them for one minute instead of three. Of course, three minutes of relaxing is better than one, but people can get a noticeable benefit from focusing on getting centered and relaxed in just one minute.

It will be important to pay attention to how these techniques affect you now when you give them less time.

Here is one more relaxation method to the list, and it involves stretching.

1 minute Relaxation – Quick Stretch

BREATHE IN—Reach up tall above your head.

BREATHE OUT—Reach down low to the floor by your toes from the waist (just as far as is comfortable for you).

BREATHE IN—Reach up to the sky again.

BREATHE OUT—Return your hands to your side.

Repeat 3-4 times.

Do the stretch routine now. Pay attention to how it affects your level of mind and body relaxation.

Do one minute of your favorite relaxation method that you have been experimenting with recently. Pay attention to its affect on you.

How would you assess the differential affect of these methods?

As you imagine trying to use them in a real situation (e.g. you see a difficult racial conversation coming, and briefly excuse yourself), what is your initial impression about the pros and cons of each method?

Through the rest of the week, try to practice at least one method twice and day. Take note of its effect on you.

Part 2: Practice Your Racial Progress Story, a Transition, and Your Unconscious Bias Story

In a few days, you are going to tell your unconscious bias and racial progress stories to others and notice what effect the stories have on them and on you. Today, you will practice them in the mirror.

The first time you will practice these steps, use the long version of the anecdote (suggested between 2 and 2.5 minutes). The second time, do the short version (suggested at about 45 seconds).

The sequence is below.

1. Say out loud something close to the following:

"One thing not talked about enough is that I think there has been an improvement in racism over the decades. "

2. Tell your racial progress story.

3. Say out loud something close to this:

"Even though there has been improvement, I also think that racism is still an issue. In fact, sometimes I still see how racial bias is something that I see actively happening in my social circle."

4. Then tell your unconscious bias story.

5) Close and synthesize the imaginary conversation by saying something like this:

"Maybe it's possible that both things are true. Racism is better than it used to be and is also still a problem that we should think about."

Reflections

How did it feel to tell the stories? Was your comfort level related to the subject or the duration of the story?

Any other takeaways from the exercise today?

Day 15
Listening Attentively

Date   /   /

"The greatest gift you can give another is the purity of your attention."
—Richard Moss

Today, you will experiment with a new type of Listening Tip. You will also use the tip in a conversation about racism with someone who is NOT likely to disagree with you about it.

> **Today's Objective**
> - Begin experimenting with a new type of Listening Tip.
> - Use that Listening Tip after asking someone to answer a question about their views of racism.

The following list of Listening Tips, potentially useful both before and during a difficult conversation, focus on how you can improve your listening by managing your own background thoughts.

1. Remind yourself that just because you listen empathetically to a point of view does not mean that you agree with it.

2. Tell yourself to listen for experiences that may be similar to ones you have had.

3. Consciously listen for potential openings for future conversations.

4. Remind yourself to listen for the underlying needs that are behind statements you hear.

5. Notice things that make the two of you similar to each other as well as things that you can agree on.

Choose two techniques you think have the best chance of working for you. If there are some other technique that works better for you, include it.

Signify which ones you have chosen.

1.

2.

Compassionate Warrior Boot Camp

Day 15

Part 2

Today, you will ask a white person about their views on whether they think that racism against people of color is a specific problem that needs specific attention or whether they think racism against all people is equally important. It is best if you choose someone who you think or know would agree with you that racism against POC is a more serious problem. Put differently, your goal is to choose someone who you have strong reason to believe is an ally, the way that this initiative has been using that term.

Your goal is to have them express their answer, then to ask them for a personal experience related to how they see it. Sometime during this encounter, you will engage one of the Listening Tips. Your goal is also to listen to them in a way that makes them feel heard.

If this feels uncomfortable and you want to tell them that you are in process of developing your listening skills, do that. But you will have a better test of your conversational skills if you do not reveal this. If possible, do not reveal that you are working on a skill—try to approach this as a natural conversation you initiated out of curiosity.

If they ask you for your perspective on the issue, tell them that you will get back to them at another time, because you want to really think about what they said. If they seem uncomfortable or insist, just answer the question naturally, perhaps using your story about witnessing unconscious bias. If possible, though, try to end the conversation with your attention on their story and your having expressed some gratitude for their sharing it.

If you wind up telling your unconscious bias story, note that it will function as a Connect story, since you and the person agree racism remains a problem. In the upcoming days, we will return to the way that the a racial progress story will likely be a Connect story for a skeptic and an Expand story for an ally. Similarly, your unconscious bias story will be an Expand story for an skeptic and a Connect story for an ally.

If the person is a skeptic AND insists that you tell them your perspective, tell them your story about how you feel racism has diminished over time.

Write down two possibilities for whom you might engage on this topic today:

1.

2.

As soon as you can after the encounter, answer the following questions:

1. How smooth or awkward was your question about their beliefs?

   ☐ Very Smooth | ☐ Smooth | ☐ Kinda Smooth/Kinda Clunky | ☐ Clunky | ☐ Very Clunky

2. How smooth was your question that transitioned them from belief to experience?

   ☐ Very Smooth | ☐ Smooth | ☐ Kinda Smooth/Kinda Clunky | ☐ Clunky | ☐ Very Clunky

Compassionate Warrior Boot Camp

48 | Day 15

3. How well do you think you listened?

    ☐ Very well | ☐ Pretty well | ☐ Ok | ☐ Not great | ☐ Pretty poorly

4. How much do you think they felt heard? They

    ☐ Felt very heard | ☐ Felt heard | ☐ Felt kinda heard | ☐ Did not feel heard

Reflections

How did it feel to approach a conversation(s) with a focus on listening?

How did the experience of engaging people in this way compared to what you expected?

1. Who was the person and what were the circumstances?

2. Which Listening Tip did you use and how/when did you use it?

3. How smooth/awkward were your opening question and your experience question?

4. How well did you listen? What were the driving forces behind how well you did?

Note: On Boot Camp Day 28 the task will be to have an Apologetic Non-Apology encounter—preferably with a skeptic in your circle. Think about whether you need to start engineering this encounter if you only interact with this person infrequently. If so, this may be a good time to start reaching out to them to re-awaken your communication channel. This will make your doing the ANA seem less out of place.

Also, on Boot Camp Day 24, your task will involve an encounter with your boot camp buddy. If you need to give them the heads up about talking that day, do so.

Compassionate Warrior Boot Camp

Date / /

Day 16
Reflection And Synthesis

"Zen masters say you cannot see your reflection in running water, only in still water." —Elizabeth Gilbert

Every seven boot camp days, it is useful to review and assess progress.

Today's Objective
Create written answers to the following questions.

Background

The path toward increased competency includes frequent pauses to reflect, assess, and make needed adjustments. The central question is:

What were your top takeaways from the past seven days of boot camp activities?

One way to get at that question is to specifically reflect upon each of the skills you have been working on. Over the past several boot camp days, what are your lessons learned and reflections used before:

Your relaxation practices?	
Your listening inclinations and skills?	
Your relationships with racism skeptics?	
Your ability/willingness to search for agreement with those whose views you disagree with?	
Your confidence in your storytelling?	
Your perspective on unconscious bias?	
Your perspective on racial progress?	
Are there notable insights that you want to keep in mind as your progress continues?	

Compassionate Warrior Boot Camp

Day 17
Asking For The Experience Of A Skeptic

"The greatest compliment that was ever paid me was when one asked me what I thought, and attended to my answer." —Henry David Thoreau

Today is the first day where, having augmented your compassion tools of Listening Tips and skills in asking experience questions, you are going to purposely engage in a conversation with someone who likely disagrees with you about racism.

> ### Today's Objective
> To practice an Ask with someone likely to have a view about racism that you disagree with.

Background

You have already practiced your relaxation method, asking about experience, attentively listening, and not expressing your perspective. Today, the goal is to do that with someone you predict will have rather different views of racial issues than you.

Preparation

Think about whom you will engage and how you might create the best atmosphere for the encounter—for yourself and for them.

Plan to do the one-minute relaxation method just before your conversation.

Choose a Listening Tip. Pick one you think would be most effective in this situation.

If it would make you more relaxed, give them the heads up that you are doing this as part of an effort to work on your listening.

If you do this, it may be helpful to mention that you have been engaging many people with many different viewpoints. If possible, just approach this as a natural conversation.

If possible, choose someone with whom you HAVE NOT had a difficult race conversation in the past.

Execution

1. Tell them you would like to have a short conversation about something that you have been thinking about.
2. Ask them if they think that racism has changed enough so that it equally affects all groups or whether it still affects traditionally disadvantaged groups more than others.

Compassionate Warrior Boot Camp

3. After they answer the question, ask them for a recent or formative experience that shapes their view. At some point, paraphrase what they said to confirm that you understood it.

4. Thank them for sharing their experience.

Additional Notes

As before, if they try to draw your views out, tell them that you will get back to them at a later point.

If demurring on the question would make your relationship awkward, tell them that you think that racism has declined, and tell them your racial progress story.

If you do this, get out of the conversation while signaling that there is more to discuss later, and you may want to come back to this topic.

Assessment

As soon as possible after the conversation, take a solitary moment to make some mental notes about.

- The questions you used to spark the conversation
- How well you listened
- The effectiveness of the relaxation techniques and the Listening Tips
- How well you closed the conversation
- How the process felt

Reflections

Who was the person and what were the circumstances?

Which Listening Tip did you use and how/when did you use it?

How smooth/awkward were your opening question and your experience question? What could have been better, if anything?

☒ Very Smooth | ☐ Smooth | ☐ Kinda Smooth/Kinda Clunky | ☐ Clunky | ☐ Very Clunky

How well did you listen? What were the driving forces behind how well you did?

☐ Very well | ☐ Well | ☐ OK | ☐ Not great | ☐ Poorly

How did the entire interaction make you feel? What are your takeaways from the experience?

Compassionate Warrior Boot Camp

Date / /

Day 18
Preparing An Apologetic Non-Apology For Two Skeptics

"Apologizing does not always mean you're wrong and the other person is right. It just means you value your relationship more than your ego."
—Mark Matthews

Before the end of the boot camp, you will have attempted to reset your communication with someone with whom you have previously had a difficult conversation about race. Today you will prepare an Apologetic Non-Apology for two different racism skeptics.

> **Today's Objective**
> Prepare the ANA for two racism skeptics in your circle.

Background

Your goal is to think about two people who are racism skeptics with whom you have had at least a somewhat unpleasant moment in a conversation about race. Hopefully, you have reasonable access to them, even if only by telephone—but in person is much, much better. Before the boot camp ends, you will actually use the ANA in a conversation with at least one of them.

Preparation

Name of Skeptic #1:

Where and when was the difficult conversation about race, and what was the topic?

What did you think or do that was unhelpful to your connection?

How could you describe what you did in a way that is honest but not off-putting ?
(For instance, saying "I thought of you as an idiot" is honest, but probably not helpful.)

As you imagine talking to them about this, how do you think you will feel?

Compassionate Warrior Boot Camp

What is an honest statement you can make about what you don't want to do again?

How would you phrase an experience question if you wanted to open the topic again?

Name of Skeptic #2:

Where and when was the difficult conversation about race, and what was the topic?

What did you think or do that was unhelpful to your connection?

How could you describe what you did in a way that is honest but not off-putting ?

As you imagine talking to them about this, how do you think you will feel?

What is an honest statement you can make about not doing this again?

How would you phrase an experience question if you wanted to open the topic again?

Execution

After you have completed the questions above, imagine you are about to have a conversation with Skeptic #1, practice one of the one-minute revelation methods, then say the Apologetic Non-Apology to the mirror. Reflect a bit on how it went, do a relaxation exercise to reset yourself, and then repeat the exercise for Skeptic #2.

As a reminder, this is the form of the Apologetic Non-Apology:

1. Recall the prior conversation and what you did or thought that was unhelpful to connectedness.

2. Say how you are feeling right now.

3. Commit to not repeating the mistake; confirm that it's okay to ask experience questions on the topic

Compassionate Warrior Boot Camp

Day 18

An example is below:

> A few months back we were talking about poverty, and I was recalling that conversation recently. I realized that during that conversation <u>I talked over you a lot</u>. I have to admit that I am <u>somewhat nervous</u> just bringing this up now. I want to say that <u>I don't plan to do that</u> in the future, and I want to say that if we ever talk about that topic again, <u>I will try to ask you about what you have seen</u> that makes you see the situation like you do. Is that all right?

Reflections

What was your emotional reaction as you answered the preparation question? Was it different for the two skeptics?

How did it feel to practice the ANA in the mirror? Was there a difference in how the mirror practice exercise felt with respect to the two skeptics?

How easy or difficult is it to imagine actually doing the ANA with these people?

Any other reflections about the exercise?

Day 19
Finding Ideas You Agree With Embedded Within Racially Problematic Statements

Date / /

> *"Diplomacy is listening to what the other guy needs. Preserving your own position, but listening to the other guy. You have to develop relationships with other people so when the tough times come, you can work together."* —Colin Powell

As you ramp up to engage skeptics, it is valuable to practice the skill of what was previously called "finding the chocolate in the trail mix." Today's task builds on the work that you did on Day 6, when you took in news stories from a perspective that you disagree with.

To further develop your ability to do this when people say things when you don't expect, you will practice on racially problematic statements that you hear now and then.

Today's Objective
To find ideas you can agree with that are embedded within racially problematic statements you disagree with.

Background

On Day 1, you wrote down several racially problematic statements that you sometimes hear and that bother you. The core task today is to review those statements and think about ideas embedded within them that you might be able to agree with.

Return to Day 1: Review your notes on the skeptics you spoke with and their statements that bother you.

Step 1: Review and re-copy your racially problematic statements from Day 1 below. If this statement came from a specific skeptic in your circle, make a note of that. At first, don't worry about writing down the "but I do agree" statements. We will come back to that.

1. I don't agree with this the idea that: (rewrite a condensed version of Statement 1 below)

but I do agree that:

Compassionate Warrior Boot Camp

2. I don't agree with this the idea that: (rewrite a condensed version of Statement 2 below)

but I do agree that:

3. I don't agree with this the idea that: (rewrite a condensed version of Statement 3 below)

but I do agree that:

4. I don't agree with the idea that: (rewrite a condensed version of Statement 4 below)

but I do agree that:

Your goal is to find an appropriate rejoinder to a racially problematic statement. Find one that you actually believe and that a skeptic would likely agree with. Two examples of appropriate rejoinders are:

Example 1	Example 2
I don't believe in the idea that:	I don't believe in the idea that:
Very few people are racist any more.	*Every group gets treated fairly by law enforcement.*
But I do agree that:	But I do agree that:
Racism has diminished a lot.	*There are many good cops on the street.*

Notice that your existing racial progress story is appropriate for Example 1. Also notice that the racial progress story would be only a marginally appropriate rejoinder for the second statement about police mistreatment. The rejoinder provided above is much more targeted to the actual statement.

Compassionate Warrior Boot Camp

Of the statements that you wrote down, make an assessment of how well your racial progress story would act as an appropriate rejoinder.

The goal of the exercise is to clarify rejoinder statements for at least two of the racially problematic statements that you took note of on Day 1. It will be a useful mental exercise to think about rejoinders for all four statements.

Once you have identified rejoinders for at least two of the statements, think about which statements seem most suitable for you to create an anecdote around. Make some notes about which rejoinders you think would provide the most fertile ground for a personal anecdote that you could create.

You will come back to these notes during the last two days of the boot camp.

Look at the statements to see if your existing Connect and Expand stories might be appropriate responses to the statement by the skeptics if they were to express such sentiments again.

Make a note of which skeptics you now have a road-map for a conversation after the boot camp is over.

If the statement does not map well onto your existing stories, review the list of statements you made for what you believe. For each one, explore how easy it might be to create a story of a formative or recent experience that animates what you do believe.

Put an asterisk by the two statements that it would be most easy to form a story around.

You will come back to this on the last day of boot camp, when you will chart future activities that you will take without daily coaching of this boot camp.

Bonus:

Find another person who you think is likely to be an ally, and repeat the exercise from yesterday. Like yesterday, vary the order in which you deliver your stories depending on how they answer your inquiry about their perspective.

Note: on Day 25, the task is to create an ANA encounter, preferably with one of your skeptics. If you need to take special measures so that you can have an encounter with this person, it may be useful to start taking those steps.

Reflections

How did you feel about looking for something you could agree with that was embedded within the racially problematic statements? If there was a part of you that wanted to avoid the exercise, what are the lessons learned from noticing this part of you?

Look back at which statements you "found the chocolate" for? Focus on the embedded ideas you jotted down. Try to think of the core subject of a personal story that illustrates your belief in the idea. Make a short note to yourself about the memory you might be able to build anecdote.

Are there any skeptics in your circle who have said the problematic statements that you may have a rejoinder for? If so, you may be able to create a strategy for talking to those skeptics based on further developing your Connect story they can agree with and an Expand story that will subsequently challenge them.

Compassionate Warrior Boot Camp

Day 20
Tell Your Stories To An Ally

"There's always room for a story that can transport people to another place." —J.K. Rowling

Today, you will go through the steps of the RACE method; your goal is to do the method in a conversation with someone that you know or think is an anti-racism ally. The best way to do this is NOT TO TELL them that you are doing an exercise in your communications skills, but rather to just tell these stories as part of a conversation.

Today's Objective
- Initiate a conversation about race with someone you predict is an ally.
- Follow the RACE method, including telling your racial progress and unconscious bias stories.

Background

The goal for today is to manage a conversation with an ally using the RACE method.

Think about one or two people you are likely to see today who you are confident is an ally—in the broad sense that they think racism against POC is a bigger problem than racism against white people.

Execution

1. Open the conversation by asking if racism against POC remains a problem needing attention. Before you do this, do a relaxation method and identify a Listening Tip you will use.

2. Whatever they say, ask them for an experience that animates their view. Listen attentively and make them feel heard.

3. If they respond as an ally (racism against POC is a bigger problem), tell them your unconscious bias story, which will serve as a Connect story, since it aligns with what they think. If you guessed wrong, and they are a skeptic, tell them your racial progress story. This will also function as a Connect story.

4. After you finish your story, transition to another story. For an ally, this will be your racial progress story. For a skeptic, this will be your unconscious bias story.

5. If it feels right, close the conversation by offering that both things could be true: Racism could be diminished and it could still be a big problem.

Doing the reflection is particularly important today, since it was your first day doing the full RACE method.

Compassionate Warrior Boot Camp

Day 20 | 59

Reflections

Which relaxation method did you use? How well did it work?

Which Listening Tip did you use? How well did it work?

How would you rate you're success in making the person feel heard? They:

☐ Felt very heard | ☐ Felt heard | ☐ Felt kinda heard | ☐ Did not feel heard

How smooth was your questioning about their point of view and experience? Why?

☐ Very Smooth | ☐ Smooth | ☐ Kinda Smooth/Kinda Clunky | ☐ Clunky | ☐ Very Clunky

How smooth was your transition to your Connect story, and how well did you tell execute it? Why?

☐ Very Smooth | ☐ Smooth | ☐ Kinda Smooth/Kinda Clunky | ☐ Clunky | ☐ Very Clunky

How smooth was your transition to your Expand story, and how well did you execute it? Why?

☐ Very Smooth | ☐ Smooth | ☐ Kinda Smooth/Kinda Clunky | ☐ Clunky | ☐ Very Clunky

How did your close the encounter?

What are your takeaways from this experience?

Compassionate Warrior Boot Camp

Date / /

Day 21
Develop A Second Set Of Unconscious Bias And Racial Progress Stories

"The story–from Rumpelstiltskin to War and Peace–is one of the basic tools invented by the human mind for the purpose of understanding. There have been great societies that did not use the wheel, but there have been no societies that did not tell stories." -Ursula K. Le Guin

Today's Objective
To begin working on two additional stories – one about racial progress and one about about unconscious bias

Background

You will come across as more natural in encounters with skeptics if you are not retelling the same anecdotes all of the time. Thus, it is important to expand your toolkit and create some additional anecdotes that you can deploy in the right moment. The goal of today is to develop two additional anecdotes and practice them in the mirror.

Before the end of the boot camp, you will have two stories about racial progress stories and two stories about unconscious bias. The stories that you will develop today will be referred to as "Batch #2" stories, in contrast to the Batch #1 stories you already have worked on.

Preparation

As stated before, it is OK – but not preferred - to tell second hand stories, especially from someone you know well and trust. If you have a friend of color who has talked about the way that racism has declined, it might be very useful to deploy this anecdote. Similarly, if you have a white friend who has told you about a moment when they noticed themselves having racially biased thoughts, this story may be very useful to you.

Two points about secondhand stories:

1. It is vital that you are able to truly inhabit the story. When you are getting the story from your source, get enough information so that you can tell it almost as if it happened to you.

2. As you think about what memories might be useful anecdotes, remember what might be credible to your audience. A secondhand story from a POC about being the recipient of unconscious bias needs to be compelling, because a skeptic's inclination will be to question the perceptions of the POC at the heart of the story. Similarly, an ally would be not inclined to trust a secondhand story about a white person thinking that racism has declined. Such a story would need to be very compelling to be useful

Compassionate Warrior Boot Camp

Day 21

Think about whether you have been told a secondhand story related to racial progress or unconscious bias that might be useful for your Compassionate Warrior toolkit. It is OK to call someone and bring up this story, have the retell it, and take notes about it. You can ask them if they would prefer that you not attach their name to the story if you retell it.

Execution

Part 1: Preparing your Batch #2 story on racial progress

- Review the description of the core elements of an anecdote on from Day 13.

- Review the prompt questions from Day 12. Review the notes you took in response to the prompt questions, adding new ones if other memories come to mind.

- After reviewing your old and new notes, get clear on one episode(s) that you will develop into an Batch #2 anecdote illustrating that there has been racial progress in recent decades. Focus on turning this memory into a usable anecdote.

What is the Set up?

What is the key moment?

What is the takeaway?

Part 2: Preparing your Batch #2 story on unconscious bias

- Review your notes from Day 7. Look for what might be a the basis of an second anecdote different than the one you already have.

What is the Set up?

Compassionate Warrior Boot Camp

Day 21

What is the key moment?

What is the takeaway?

Part 3: Mirror Practice

After you have developed your anecdotes, practice them in the mirror.

Reflections:

Did you have any notable reactions to the assignment of coming up with additional stories?

Does the idea of developing additional stories seem closer to exciting or more headaches?

Do you have any reaction to the idea of learning about and telling second hand stories?

Date / /

Day 22
Reflection And Synthesis

"It's on the strength of observation and reflection that one finds a way. So we must dig and delve unceasingly." —Claude Monet

You have practiced the RACE method and begun to expand your toolkit even further. Before you push your skill set out even more, it is useful to take stock.

> **Today's Objective**
> Create written answers to the questions listed below.

Background

The path toward increased competency includes frequent pauses to reflect, assess, and make needed adjustments. The central question is:

What were your top takeaways from the past seven days of boot camp activities?

One way to get at that question is to specifically reflect on each of the skills that you have been practicing.

Reflections

Over the past boot camp days, what are your lessons learned and reflections about:

- Your relaxation practices?

- Your skill in asking questions that transition from beliefs to experience?

- Your listening inclinations and skills?

Compassionate Warrior Boot Camp

Day 22

- Your relationships with racism skeptics?

- Your ability/willingness to search for agreement with those whose views you disagree with?

- Your confidence in your story telling? How has it changed over the past week of boot camp days? What have your learned about how to be more effective?

- Your perspective on unconscious bias?

- Your perspective on racial progress?

Are there notable insights that you want to keep in mind as you progress to the next week?

Compassionate Warrior Boot Camp

Day 23
RACE Method With Batch #2 Stories To An Ally

"The more you leave out, the more you highlight what you leave in."
—Henry Green

Your goal today and tomorrow is to get some practice in telling your second Connect and Expand stories to someone who you anticipate looks at racism largely the same as you do.

> ### Today's Objective
> Deploy your Batch #2 racial progress and unconscious bias stories with someone you predict will be an ally.

Background

Your skills in storytelling in the service of allyship will always be growing. In addition, there will always be the first time you tell your story in service of wielding influence. Today, you will use your 2nd Batch of stories (created on boot camp Day 21) while using the RACE method with an ally.

The following instructions are a repeat of Day 20, except that you will use your 2nd Batch racial progress and unconscious bias stories. If you were not able to create those, then do the RACE method with a different ally than before.

A possible alteration that you might make is varying your relaxation methods and Listening Tips and paying attention to how they affect you.

Execution

1. Open the conversation by asking if racism against POC remains a problem needing attention. Before you do this, do a relaxation method and identify a Listening Tip you will use.

2. Whatever they say, ask them for experience that animates their view. Listen attentively and make them feel heard.

3. If they respond as an ally (racism against POC is a bigger problem), tell them your unconscious bias story. This will serve as a Connect story, since it aligns with what they think. If they are a skeptic, tell them your racial progress story. This will function as a Connect story.

4. After you finish your story, transition to other story. For an ally, this will be your racial progress story. For a skeptic, this will be your unconscious bias story.

5. If it feels right, close the conversation by offering that both things could be true—racism could be diminished, and it could still be a big problem.

Compassionate Warrior Boot Camp

Day 23

Reflections

Which relaxation method did you use? How well did it work?

Which Listening Tip did you use? How well did it work?

How would you assess how much the person felt heard? They:

[x] Felt very heard | ☐ Felt heard | ☐ Felt kinda heard | ☐ Did not feel heard

How smooth was your questioning about their point of view and experience?
☐ Very Smooth | ☐ Smooth | ☐ Kinda Smooth/Kinda Clunky | ☐ Clunky | ☐ Very Clunky

How smooth was your transition to your Connect story, and how well did you tell execute it?
☐ Very Smooth | ☐ Smooth | ☐ Kinda Smooth/Kinda Clunky | ☐ Clunky | ☐ Very Clunky

How smooth was your transition to your Expand story, and how well did you execute it?
☐ Very Smooth | ☐ Smooth | ☐ Kinda Smooth/Kinda Clunky | ☐ Clunky | ☐ Very Clunky

How did your close the encounter?

What are your big takeaways from this experience?

Compassionate Warrior Boot Camp

Day 24
Get Feedback From Your Boot Camp Buddy And ANA Role Play

Date   /   /

"In a growth mindset, challenges are exciting rather than threatening. So rather than thinking, oh, I'm going to reveal my weaknesses, you say, wow, here's a chance to grow." —Carol Dweck

Today's set of tasks is the longest in the entire boot camp. You will need about 30 minutes of the time of a boot camp buddy. The exercises will involve you practicing your stories and role playing the Apologetic Non-Apology.

Today's Objective
- Practice your stories with your boot camp buddy and get feedback.
- Do a role play with your buddy playing the role of a skeptic in your circle.

Part 1: Feedback on Your Stories

Preparation

1. Explain to your boot camp buddy that you want to get feedback on your Batch #1 and Batch #2 stories. Show them the feedback questions below.

2. Explain how the RACE method works if you haven't previously. Start with the longer version of your Batch #2 stories.

3. After you get feedback, retell the stories and attempt to integrate their feedback.

4. If possible, discuss ways you might modify the telling if you are telling it at a much shorter duration.

5. Move to the Batch #1 stories, and repeat the process.

Here are the questions that your buddy should touch on in addition to other feedback that might come to their mind.

How compelling is the story?

How well do you draw the listener in as you tell it?

Are there any nuances or subtleties that are likely to generate resistance or engagement by racism skeptics?

How smooth or awkward is your transition between the stories? Is there any way to improve it?

Compassionate Warrior Boot Camp

Part 2: Apologetic Non-Apology Role-Play

On Day 15, you prepared the ANA for one or two people with whom you have had a difficult racial conversation. Today, you will build on that preparation and do a role play with your ally partner playing the role of the skeptics. This will work MUCH better in-person than if you do this on the telephone or through the computer. However, either of those is superior to you just imagining talking to the skeptic and talking to the mirror, which you have already done.

> Here is the conversation sequence:
>
> **You:** Nice to see you again, friend.
>
> **Friend:** *(played by your boot camp buddy)*: Nice to see you.
>
> **You:** I have been thinking about a conversation we had a while back. Can we take a second to talk about it?
>
> **Friend:** Sure.
>
> **You:** *(you will execute the ANA),*
>
> **You:** Remember when were talking about *(the topic)*?
>
> **Friend:** Yes
>
> **You:** I was thinking about it the other day, and I realized that:
>
> - **(Part 1 – Accountability for the Past)** I was *(some description of something you did that was unhelpful to connectedness)*.
>
> - **(Part 2 – Vulnerability in the Present)** Even now as I talk about it, I am feeling *(how you think you will feel)*.
>
> - **(Part 3 – Commitment to Better Behavior and More Questions in the Future)** So I want to say that if we talk about this again, I am committed to not doing that. And if we speak of this again, I want to ask you about your experiences related to this. Is that okay?
>
> **Friend:** Yes

After this, debrief the experience with your friend. Answer these questions:

- How did each you feel about the exercise?

- What adjustments need to be made with respect to what you can expect to feel when you actually talk to the skeptic?

- Are there any other lessons that you should take away?

In addition, give your friend a moment to comment on the process.

Do the same exercise again, focusing on a different skeptic.

Reflections on Part 1: Feedback on Stories

Did anything your boot camp buddy said about your stories surprise you?

How successful were you in making adjustments based on feedback? Were there adjustments that you found yourself resisting?

Do you favor any of your four stories over the others? Why? Do you have thoughts about which to deploy in what situations?

What other guidelines/lessons should you keep in mind as you make decisions about using these stories as you attempt to influence people?

Reflections on Part 2: ANA Role Play

What lessons do you take from this process?

How did you feel during the process compared how you thought you would feel?

Having done this, do you want to change the topic or change the skeptic you will approach before the end of the boot camp?

Date / /

Day 25
RACE Method With An Ally, Choosing Between Stories

"Only he who is well prepared has any opportunity to improvise."
—*Ingmar Bergman*

Today you will use the RACE method with an ally. Unlike recent boot camp days, you will make a choice in the moment on which racial progress and unconscious bias story to tell. This will push you one more step toward being able to flexibly manage a conversation with a skeptic.

Today's Objective
- To have a conversation with a likely ally using the RACE method.
- To make a choice in the moment about which two of your four stories you will use.

Background

The goal of this initiative is not to make you a robot but rather a fluid manager of productive conversation. Improvisational thinking is important. At this point, you have practiced both sets of your stories more than once. Today's task is to have a conversation with an ally where you decide in the moment which anecdotes you will share.

Preparation

Make a mental plan about which ally in your circle you will engage today.

Review the main points of all of your stories.

Remind yourself that you are choosing someone with whom you likely agree about racial issues.

If possible, do not tell the person that this conversation is part of a class you are taking. If you can, just approach it as a regular conversation.

Execution

1. Just before your encounter, do a relaxation method and choose a Listening Tip.

2. Open the conversation by asking their perspective about racism, as you have previously during the boot camp.

3. Listen empathetically, making sure they feel heard. Notice how well your Listening Tip works for you.

4. Choose whichever story feels right for your Connect story. *(If this person is an ally, it will be one of your racial progress stories.)* You do not have to keep the stories in the pair that you developed them.

Compassionate Warrior Boot Camp

5. Shortly after the encounter, take a moment to make some mental or written notes.

Feel free to congratulate yourself for in some way that feels appropriate. You have made a big step forward!

Reflections

- Which relaxation method did you use? How well did it work?

- Which Listening Tip did you use? How well did it work?

- How would you rate your listening?

- How smooth was your questioning about their point of view and experience? What made it that way?
  ☐ Very Smooth | ☐ Smooth | ☐ Kinda Smooth/Kinda Clunky | ☐ Clunky | ☐ Very Clunky

- How smooth was your transition to your Connect story, and how well did you tell it?
  ☐ Very Smooth | ☐ Smooth | ☐ Kinda Smooth/Kinda Clunky | ☐ Clunky | ☐ Very Clunky

- How smooth was your transition to your Expand story, and how well did you tell it?
  ☐ Very Smooth | ☐ Smooth | ☐ Kinda Smooth/Kinda Clunky | ☐ Clunky | ☐ Very Clunky

- How did your close the encounter?

- What are your big takeaways from this experience?

- Upon reflection, would you choose the same stories for both Connect and Expand. Why or why not?

- What adjustments would you make any point in the sequence?

Date   /   /

Day 26
RACE Method With An Ally, Choosing Between Stories, After Adjustments

"The pursuit of perfection often impedes improvement." —George Will

Today is the last practice day with the RACE method before you purposely use it to engage a skeptic.

Today's Objective
- Review the adjustments that you said were important to consider from Day 25.
- Engage someone you anticipate is an ally, and implement the RACE method, making an improvisational choice about which stories to use.

Background

The primary difference between today and Day 25 is that you have a chance to make adjustments based on your own reflections from the previous experience. Consider trying different relaxation methods and Listening Tips.

Go into the encounter with a plan to use the stories you did NOT use on Day 25. However, if something happens in the encounter that pushes you to tell one or more of the stories you used on Day 25, do what feels most suitable.

Preparation

Make a mental plan about which ally in your circle you will engage today.

Review the main points of all your stories.

Remind yourself that you are choosing someone with whom you likely agree about racial issues.

If possible, do not tell the person that this conversation is part of a class you are taking. If you can, just approach it as a regular conversation.

Execution

1. Just before your encounter, do a relaxation method and choose a Listening Tip.
2. Open the conversation by asking their perspective about racism, as you have previously done.
3. Listen empathetically, making sure they feel heard. Notice how well your Listening Tip works.
4. Plan to use the stories you DID NOT use on Day 25, but let the situation dictate your final choice.
5. Shortly after the encounter, take a moment to make some mental or written notes.

Compassionate Warrior Boot Camp

Day 26

Reflections

Which relaxation method did you use? How well did it work?

Which Listening Tip did you use? How well did it work

How would you rate your listening?

How smooth was your questioning about their point of view and experience? What made it this way?
☐ Very Smooth | ☐ Smooth | ☐ Kinda Smooth/Kinda Clunky | ☐ Clunky | ☐ Very Clunky

How smooth was your transition to your Connect story, and how well did you tell it?
☐ Very Smooth | ☐ Smooth | ☐ Kinda Smooth/Kinda Clunky | ☐ Clunky | ☐ Very Clunky

How smooth was your transition to your Expand story, and how well did you tell it?
☐ Very Smooth | ☐ Smooth | ☐ Kinda Smooth/Kinda Clunky | ☐ Clunky | ☐ Very Clunky

How did your close the encounter?

What are your big takeaways from this experience?

Upon reflection, would you choose the same stories for both Connect and Expand. Why or why not?

What adjustments would you make to what you did at any point in the sequence?

Compassionate Warrior Boot Camp

Day 27
RACE Method With Skeptic

Date / /

"A man would do nothing, if he waited until he could do it so well that no one would find fault with what he has done." —Cardinal Newman

Today's the day! Your goal today is to deploy the RACE method with a racism skeptic. Even though there are more days left the boot camp, if you do today's tasks, you will have essentially graduated. The other days will be like senior week, after you have aced final exams.

> **Today's Objective**
> Successfully deploy RACE method with someone who is a racism skeptic.

Background

ACT defines a successful encounter with a racism skeptic as one where you get to be yourself for some or all of the interaction, and they leave the conversation not being completely disinterested in talking to you about race at some future point.

You are in a strong position to create an effective encounter. You have practiced how to center yourself, how to ask experience questions, and how to listen. You have also developed and practiced two Connect stories about racism diminishing and two Expand stories about your being a witness to racial bias.

You got this.

Preparation

Choose the skeptic you hope to engage, as well as a backup skeptic. It may make sense not to choose the most hardened racist you know. To lessen the risk of your being triggered and thrown off center, make a plan to engage someone whose views bother you, not someone whose views your abhor.

Before you approach them, do a relaxation method. Remind yourself of your Listening Tip.

Execution

- Use whatever conversation openers you think will engage them while not putting them on the defensive. Consider that they may be expecting you to judge them.

- As you go through the Ask, Connect, and Expand steps, pay attention to how well you are executing the method as well as the impact on them.

- Pause to reflect and assess as soon as you can after the encounter. Take some mental or written notes.

Other important things to remember: Approach the conversation with a strategy, but have flexibility. This applies to your stories for instance, or the ways that you will attempt to create a sense of connection in other ways.

Compassionate Warrior Boot Camp

Day 27

Reflection

Which relaxation method did you use? How well did it work?

Which Listening Tip did you use? How well did it work?

How would you rate your listening?

How smooth was your questioning about their point of view and experience?

How smooth was your transition to your Connect story, and how well did you tell it?

How smooth was your transition to your Expand story, and how well did you tell it?

How did your close the encounter?

What are your big takeaways from this experience?

Upon reflection, would you choose the same stories for both the Connect and Expand steps. Why or why not?

Compassionate Warrior Boot Camp

Day 28
RACE Method With A Skeptic, After Adjustments

Date   /   /

> *"Success may require a lot of days. But progress only requires one."*
> —T. Jay Taylor

The goal today is to execute the RACE method again, making adjustments you have assessed will help your effectiveness.

Today's Objective
- Clarify opportunities for improvement from your performance on Day 26.
- Execute the RACE method, making the adjustments you intended.

Background

Your goal today is essentially the same as Day 27—to engage a conversation with someone who you assess beforehand is a racism skeptic. Before you do that, you will take some notes on possible improvements from Day 27. The goal is to try to implement those improvements, and note the success of your attempt.

By making an adjustment today, you will further solidify in your spirit that what you are doing is a personal practice you are attending to and moving slowly toward mastery over. Both of these are useful to experience as this boot camp ends and you not propelled with today's instruction.

Preparation

Take some notes on possible adjustments you might make to each sub-task within the RACE method.

Here are some changes that I plan to make when I deploy the RACE method today.

Subtask	Adjustment I will make
Relaxing before the encounter	
Choosing a Listening Tip	
Asking a question about experience	
Connect—telling a story the person likely agrees with	
Expand telling a story that will invite the person to new thinking	

Compassionate Warrior Boot Camp

Assessment

Which relaxation method did you use? How well did it work?

Which Listening Tip did you use? How well did it work

How would you rate your listening?

How smooth was your questioning about their point of view and experience?

How smooth was your transition to your Connect story, and how well did you tell it?

How smooth was your transition to your Expand story, and how well did you tell it?

How did your close the encounter?

What are your big takeaways from this experience?

Upon reflection, would you choose the same stories for both Connect and Expand. Why or why not?

If you planned to make any adjustments on any of the above, make a note of the degree to which you executed the adjustments and what happened.

Compassionate Warrior Boot Camp

Day 29
Executing An Apologetic Non-Apologetic

"When you forgive, you free your soul. But when you say I'm sorry, you free two souls." —Donald L. Hicks

Since early in the Boot Camp, you have been working toward doing an Apologetic Non-Apology. For the past two boot camp days, the task has been to do the RACE method with someone who you may not have experienced a disconnection around race before. Today you will do the ANA, and depending on your choices in the moment, you might further the reconciliation by doing the entire RACE method.

Today's Objective
- To rehearse the ANA in the mirror.
- To talk to a skeptic you have a healed relationship with and deploy the ANA.

Background

The goal of the ANA is to use a past tough conversation about race as a springboard to not only heal a relationship but also improve potential future conversations about race or about other issues.

One feature of deploying the ANA is that you can make strategic choices about how far you want the interaction to go.

Specifically, the core part of the ANA ends with you letting the person know that if you talk about the topic again, you want to 1) not repeat the bad thing you did before and 2) ask them about their experiences related to the topic.

After you deliver the ANA soliloquy, you have will likely have at least three options.

Option 1: Signal that you feel the exchange has been completed, and exit the conversation. This is a perfectly reasonable choice, especially since you just told them you are feeling at least a bit vulnerable. Note that you have the option of re-opening the previous conversation about the topic, but you don't have to.

Option 2: Reopen the conversation partially. If you want to, you can build on the permission they have granted to ask about their experience, and ask them about their experience. It is also possible that they will launch into discussing their point of view without being asked. If they talk about their opinion, redirect them to their experience that drives their opinion.

If they just start giving their experience that drives their opinion, you are in a good position to attentively listen, since you have been practicing this through the boot camp.

After they tell their experience, you can thank them and exit the conversation. If they seem like they want to be combative, or the topic is far afield from stories you have, or for any other reason, you can say you want to percolate on their story and exit the conversation.

Option 3: If it feels like you have Connect and Expand stories suitable to the moment, you can proceed with the RACE method.

Preparation

Review your notes from Day 16, and choose which skeptic you plan to engage today. Do whatever it takes to arrange an encounter with the person.

Rehearse your ANA in the mirror.

Before and after you do this, do your favorite relaxation technique.

Remember which Listening Tip you want to use. Because this is a person you have a relationship with, there might be other listening tips that the ones you experimented with that might work better. Review days 2, 9, 15 to see all of the tips in three categories.

As you go into the encounter, made decisions about how far you think it will go. But do not get overly attached to this decision. Give yourself psychological room to push forward or or to pull back if you think you need to in the midst of the encounter.

Try to take notes about what happened as soon after the encounter as possible .

Reflections

How did you feel during the process compared to what you thought you would fear?

What appeared to be the impact of the ANA on the person?

How do you feel about your choice in the moment to go as far as you chose to take the conversation?

Overall, was there any notable change in how your relationship with this person feels?

Were there any other impacts of this experience worth noting?

Day 30
Preparing To Sustain The Journey

"If you want to go fast, go by yourself. If you want to go far, go with others" —African Proverb

> **Today's Objective**
> - Think about allies who might be useful supports to your Compassionate Warrior Practice.
> - Think about people whom you might want to tell about your boot camp experience.
> - Read the closing commentary about different ways of talking about this experience.

Background

Congratulations! You have completed an important journey of improved competence skills of deploying compassion-based strategies in the fight to dismantle racism. And you are also at the beginning of a long journey to improve your competence. Today's task is primarily one of reflection and planning for Day 31 and beyond.

Managing Your Own Journey

The nature of the ally's path is that it is optional. Anti-racism allies people choose how much energy they want to spend on dismantling racism; they can choose anywhere from "none" to "occasionally" to "every waking moment".

One factor that will most likely keep you actively engaging the ally path is to be in some regular communication with other people who look at being a better ally as an important part of their personal mission. It will be useful to identify others who would not mind talking about the quality and quantify of their efforts to be forces opposing racism.

As noted on Day 1, there are many dimensions of allyship, even though this initiative only focuses on talking to racism skeptics. At the end of today's instruction, note the form in the White Ally Toolkit Workbook that encourages you to review up to six allies in your circle. The point is to consider who might be in an ally support group that you might start.

Once you have thought about the people who would be most important as supporters to your ally journey, think about ways to structure that support. For example, you might decide on weekly text, a bi-weekly phone call, or a monthly meeting. The most important thing now is to think about the people who seem most suitable to providing mutual support on your journey toward more effective allyship.

Tools, Products, and Services

The initiative associated with this boot camp—the Ally Conversation Toolkit—is specifically designed to help anti-racism allies start and continue their journey. There is a good deal of free content on the public Facebook pages, YouTube, and allyconversationtoolkit.com. In addition, there are additional resources on communication to productively engage with racism skeptics, a weakness in American political culture becomes a little less weak. If you see your ally journey as making the nation stronger, don't be shy about talking about it in these terms.

Increasing Your Discernment About Allies Who Can Help Your Journey

It is useful to think about who are the people in your circle – defined broadly – who you might want to meet with regularly (say, bi-weekly or monthly) to talk about your influence practice.

First, think of the six folks that you are most drawn to considering for your three-person racial ally support group. Write their names here.

1.	4.
2.	5.
3.	6.

In addition to typical factors you use to choose people, the following characteristics seem of particular importance.

- Willingness to try to push oneself past limitations • Capacity to be reflective
- Graciousness to others (and themselves) when goals are not met • Level of commitment to racial equity

Next you are going to analyze your list of potential ally practice supporters. Below is a table with the four characteristics above and a blank space for criteria that you might think is particularly important, too. As you rate the ally, compare them to other people who are allies in the broad definition of that word. (That is, it is OK if they have never gone to a White Ally meeting).

Scale: 4 – really strong 1 – relatively weak	Is willing to push themselves	Capacity to reflect	Graciousness	Commitment to racial equity
Person				
1.				
2.				
3.				
4.				
5.				
6.				

In light of this exercise, people seem most suitable to recruit to actively support your journey as an ant-racism ally?

Thanks for your allyship and keep up the good work!

Compassionate Warrior Boot Camp

the subscriber page; these resources include access to other people on a similar ally journey, automated video and written resources, and access to coaching. You are invited to avail yourself of the free and subscription resources.

Of course, this initiative is not the only resource that can be helpful to allies on their journey. Appendix 1 provides a list—inherently only partial and imperfect—of other resources that you might consider making a part of your ongoing ally journey.

The Bigger Context of Your Anti-Racism Ally Practice

If you have benefited from this experience, the initiative wants you to push yourself to spread the word about it to others. Of course, everyone is not a promoter, and many allies are introverts who are disinclined to energetically promote anything. Still this guide will close with a few brief comments about how you might think about and talk about your journey toward becoming a Compassionate Warrior against racism. As you talk to other white people who may wonder why you are engaged in this practice, these other rationales may help them see that becoming actively engaged in ally work is bigger than the goal of creating more racial equity.

Personal Growth

This boot camp may have strengthened your ability to stay centered in challenging moments. Obviously, increasing your ability to stay centered is a good thing and can potentially have benefits outside of talking about racial issues. Focusing on staying centered and engaging people in ways that are based on compassion is a suggestion from spiritual teachers from almost every tradition. While this boot camp has not highlighted this work as an enhancement to your spiritual practice, it could have. This is a valid way of seeing what this work is about. Moreover, throwing more compassion in the world often has a multiplier effect, because when people receive compassion, they are more likely to extend compassion to others. If you see your anti-racism ally journey as part of a larger process of personal and collective spiritual growth, don't be shy about talking about it in these terms.

Relationships

After immersing themselves in practices of compassionate-based communication on one topic, many allies notice that it enhances their communications capacities on other issues. This improved skill, in turn, can have a healing effect on relationships, whether conflicts about race were a big or small part of those relationships. By improving your ability to engage compassionately and from a place of empathetic listening, you are likely to be a calming force countering the tensions at social gatherings that include people with whom vehemently disagree. Given the way that current public and political issues often undermine family and other relationships and things as prosaic as Thanksgiving, you may become a force for comity at such settings. If you see your anti-racism ally journey as making it easier for families and friends to get along, don't be shy about talking about it in these terms.

American Political Culture

The Ally Conversation Toolkit is specifically devoted to dismantling various "isms" (racism, sexism, homophobia, etc.) that undermine America (and every other nation, for that matter). Our inability to talk about our nation's oldest problem is related to our increasing inability to cross ideological divides. Let's remember, this inability is a national weakness that America's enemies are purposely trying to exploit for their own advantage. Any time an American learns how to purposely deploy compassion-based

Appendix | 83

Resources
Other resources to enhance your journey toward being a Compassionate Warrior

There is a growing understanding of the important role that white people can play in dismantling racism. Accordingly, there are a growing number of resources that people can avail themselves to if they want some assistance for their journey toward great insight and effectiveness in promoting racial.

This should be considered a very partial list and extremely imperfect listing of the resources that are available. While most of these tools are specifically targeted toward white allies, some of them are intended to be of use to anyone in the anti-racism movement.

Web

- **Ally Conversation Toolkit** - (www.allyconversationtoolit.com)
  This is the initiative behind this Compassionate Warrior Boot Camp. The website and initiative has a number of resources available, including the White Ally Toolkit Workbook, The Discussion Guide to the Workbook, the ACT Introductory Video Course, the Holiday Survive and Thrive Webinar. There is also Subscriber service to allow access to resources that are not available on the very resource-rich free part of the website.

- **Racial Equity Tools** – (www.racialequitytools.org)
  This very large and well-curated resource full houses a variety of research tips, tools, and curricula to help those working toward justice in systems, organizations, communities, and the culture at large.

Books

- **White Ally Toolkit Workbook, by David Campt** – (www.allyconversationtoolkit.com)
- **Living in the Tension, by Shelly Tochluk** - (www.shellytochluk.com)
- **Witnessing Whiteness, by Shelly Tochluk**
- **White Fragility by Robin DiAngelo** - www.robindiangelo.com
- **What Does it Mean to be White: Developing White Racial Literacy by Robin DiAngelo**
- **Waking up White, by Debby Irving** - (www.debbyirving.com)
- **White Like Me, by Tim Wise** – (@timjacobwise)

Guides for Regular Practice and Reflection

- **Understanding What It Means to be White and Privileged Journal, by Tom Schweizer**
- **21 Day Racial Equity Habit Building Challenge** – www.debbyirving.com/21-day-challenge/
- **Pointmade daily racial equity instagram** https://www.instagram.com/pointmadelearning/

Compassionate Warrior Boot Camp